Comments from early readers of
***End-of-Life Spiritual Care: Spiritual Insights and Biblical Rituals to Help Your Loved One Step into Eternity with Faith, Love, and Dignity,* by Rose Martin**

"I find it very well written! It offers comfort for not only the patient but the family too. This offers a spiritual and a physical way to help the patient and the family. And that's a very good thing. The family is always looking for some way to help the patient. And if it helps the patient then it helps them. Whether they do all or pick through the list and do some of the things, you not only presented them with ideas, but exactly how to do them. Awesome! - Mary Beth Willi, LPN, *Learning How to Let Go The Signs and Symptoms of the Dying Process*

"I have been savoring your book since I received it. As I read it, I'd have a question pop into my mind and the answer would appear in the next portion! This is such a Spirit Filled Book. I can just feel the tenderness with which the dying person is being treated. They are also being treated with dignity and respect. I so appreciate that you have written this book." - Debbie P.S., Missouri

"I wish I had been able to have your book when my mother died. I would have loved to do these things with her. I know it would have comforted her in the most loving way. I am going to purchase one of these books for my daughter so she can do this with me when my time comes. Never have I read such a touching, caring, comforting, and loving book to guide families through the spiritual journey of death for a loved one. I truly did love it. Thank you so much!" - Jamie F., Arkansas

MAY YOU AND YOUR LOVED ONE
BE BLESSED BY THIS BOOK!

End-of-Life Spiritual Care

is written for everyday people

who want to help

their very special loved one

step into eternity.

VISIT US AT

WWW.END-OF-LIFE-SPIRITUAL-CARE.COM

End-of-Life
Spiritual Care

End-of-Life

Spiritual Care

SPIRITUAL INSIGHTS AND BIBLICAL RITUALS TO HELP YOUR LOVED ONE STEP INTO ETERNITY WITH FAITH, LOVE, AND DIGNITY

ROSE MARTIN

ACHIEVEMENT
PUBLICATIONS
Bella Vista, AR 72715

End-of-Life Spiritual Care: Spiritual Insights and Biblical Rituals to Help Your Loved One Step into Eternity with Faith, Love, and Dignity, by Rose Martin

Book ISBN: 978-0-9643457-7-5
Library of Congress Control Number:

Published by:
Achievement Publications
PO Box 3321, Bella Vista, AR 72715, USA

Email: SpiritualCareCollection@gmail.com
Website: www.End-of-Life-Spiritual-Care.com

Edited by: Charles T. Martin

Cover by: Rose Martin
Cover Photo: © Can Stock Photo/Satori

Disclaimer Notice:
The content provided herein is for educational purposes only. At publishing time every effort has been made to ensure that the content provided is accurate and helpful for the reader. However, this is not an exhaustive coverage of the subject. The reader is responsible for his/her own life choices and decisions. These decisions are theirs to make. No liability is assumed for losses or damages due to the information provided. Purchasing this book can be seen as consent to the fact that both the publisher and the author of this book are not qualified to give legal, financial, medical, psychological, psychiatric, or any other specialist advice through a book. If you require such advice, you should seek a licensed professional or a minister. Professionals should be consulted as needed before undertaking any of the actions suggested herein. The author's service is to provide biblical spiritual end-of-life information to all people.

Dedication

This book is dedicated to my mother and my father,
Annamarie and Sigfried,
both of whose lives and deaths were instrumental
in my discovery of God, Truth, and Eternity.

"Sitting at the bedside, holding her hand. No words. The Spirit was healing and bonding us. Feeling nothing but love and that I wanted to comfort her and be with her to the end."
— A journaled note from my time with my mother at the end of her life.

Acknowledgements

I thank the Lord for giving me direction on what to do during my mother's death, and the courage to do it. I thank Him for all that He has shown me since.

I thank my father Sigfried for his role in my spiritual life. His death was the beginning of my spiritual journey, which has not stopped. May you be blessed.

I thank my mother Annamarie for her role in my spiritual life as well. Her death showed me a new level of God's love and brought the meaning of life and eternity together for me. May you be blessed.

I thank my sister Margret for being a devoted daughter and caregiver to our mother for many years, and for the love we shared helping our mother go home to the Lord.

I thank my husband Charles who is my sounding board and editor. I am thankful for his support and for helping correct the 'German accent' in my writing style.

I thank Mary Beth Willi, LPN for her booklet entitled, *Learning How to Let Go The Signs and Symptoms of the Dying Process*, that was made available to us at my mother's Hospice Center. This booklet not only taught me about the physical dying process, but also introduced me to the spiritual aspect of death. Subsequently, I thank her for her input and confirmation of the dying process spoken about in this book.

I thank the hospice nurses and those who have lost loved ones who shared their stories of the dying process. These stories helped me confirm and understand what the Spirit was teaching me.

And most of all, to the Spirit of God through Yeshua, who opened my eyes to the spiritual process of transitioning from here to eternity and showing me how it correlates with the Word of God.

I am thankful in advance for the many individuals that will read this book - that it will be a blessing to them at the time of their loved one's passing, as well as give more meaning to their own lives and the dying process.

Contents at a Glance

How this Book Came to Be...

When my sister called to tell me that our 94-year-old mother was admitted into hospice and in the final days of her life, I packed up my bags and drove 15 hours overnight to be with my mother to support her and my sister through her final days. I did not know what to expect.

My mother strongly believed in Jesus as her Savior, and as a Believer myself, a priest and king in God's Kingdom, as well as Christian Minister, I was led to include spiritual items and rituals to her transition. I believed that she also wanted this as she was a woman of faith and loved the Lord.

I brought with me my prayer scarf that our son brought back for me from his trip to Israel, my Bible, anointing oil, and a list of angels that I could call upon to help. I depended on the Holy Spirit to guide me the rest of the way.

My mother was Roman Catholic, and a few days before I arrived, we called a priest from her Parish to pray for her and give her communion and the Last Rites of her faith.

When I arrived in my mother's hospice room, I began by anointing her forehead with oil in the Name of Yeshua, Jesus. I cleansed the spiritual atmosphere of her room with prayers, decrees, and worship. My sister, my niece and nephew, and I stayed with our mother and Oma (German for grandmother). We fellowshipped with each other throughout the rest of the day and kept the rest of my family that was at a distance included and up to date as much as possible. My sister kept vigil through the night.

The next morning, my sister called me at my hotel to come to the Hospice Center, that there was a change, and our mother was very different today. When I got to my mother's room, I noticed her countenance had changed. The childish, unsure, somewhat frightened, and confused nature from the day before was gone. Her countenance was now more serene, more serious, more withdrawn.

Even though she did not speak or open her eyes much anymore you could see and sense the change. As I reflected on it later, it was as if the spiritual clutter was removed, and the clouds began to part in her understanding. What was happening became clearer to her. She was beginning to see past the veil. She began to realize what she had to do.

I placed the prayer scarf on her head. Although she had been unresponsive, she reached for the bottom of it as I put it on her head and tied it loosely under her chin. I told her it was the prayer scarf her grandson brought back from Israel. She wrapped her fingers around it and held the bottom of each side of it. It brought her security, knowing she was under the shelter of her Almighty God and had the love of her family. We kept it on her all the way through her death. I kept it afterwards, along with some other items from my mother, as a cherished memory of her transition to Heaven.

I arrived at my mother's room at the Hospice Center in the early morning hours on a Sunday. Seven days later, in the early morning hours on a Sunday my mother exhaled her last breath and died. It happened to be Easter Sunday morning! The symbolism of her dying on that particular day meant so much to us. It was the perfect ending to all the love we felt and the wonders we had experienced.

During each of those seven days I was able to spend with my mother, my sister and I prayed with and over her at her bedside and kept God's Word and promises in our thoughts and activities. The rest of our family kept her in their thoughts and prayers throughout the entire time also.

I had a lot of time to think and pray. Each day God showed me something new about His Word, life, death, and eternity. Each day the love and hope began to feel stronger. It was an amazing experience.

My mother's death was special for our entire family, for those present and those at a far distance. We all love her very much. Everyone was able to say goodbye and find peace by the time my mother exhaled her final breath and stepped into eternity, into the loving arms of God, and of her loving husband, my dad. We believe she received a warm welcome from all the loved ones that had gone before as she was the last of her friends, family, and siblings to arrive in Heaven!

In addition to the love and devotion she received from her family, the few spiritual items that I brought with me gave such comfort to my mother. They brought me comfort too, knowing that they added peace and understanding to her passing. Several nurses even marveled at what a peaceful transition it was.

Having a candle would have been a wonderful addition, but I did not think about it until it was too late. No one at the Hospice Center had any type of candle either – wax or battery – and I did not have time to go buy one. It would have been a nice touch.

I brought a notebook and pen with me so I could keep notes, which also proved valuable. There were spiritual activities going on, and some of them reminded me of a particular Scripture at once. I would write it down and reflect on it. Then I would get another and then another revelation. Afterwards I was glad I wrote things down as the days began to blur together and I would have forgotten some key moments. I did not have any real idea of what to expect ahead of time and it would have been helpful to know. Even so, it was a real blessing, discovering and experiencing it all.

My mother's passing was one of the most spiritual loving experiences of my life. I believe the acts of faith created a sacred space which contributed greatly to guiding her transition and bringing comfort to her and our entire family. They helped my mom through the labor of dying. God's love filled each of our hearts more each day.

What surprised me after all of this was, the realization that after over 36 years of studying the Word and even sitting under advanced teachings, I never came across anything about the spiritual aspect of the dying process including the all-important life review! How many other Believers have never been taught anything about this either? We only learned about going to Heaven and not much else. The spiritual process of transitioning there and what to expect was never addressed! However, at the bedside of my mother, through her labor of dying, I perceived the amazing spiritual activity that takes place when one of God's children goes home!

After this tremendously powerful spiritual experience, I felt an urgency to share with other families what I learned at my mother's bedside to help them understand more about the spiritual aspect of dying and through that insight to also bring comfort to their grieving.

I also wanted to share with individuals and families how they can richly bless their loved one in their finals days by using common spiritual items and rituals to create a sacred space for them in which to do their labor of dying. I realized that many people may not be able to have a pastor, priest, or other spiritual elder come to anoint their loved one or minister communion, so these activities would be something that the family could do together for their loved one.

I prayed for the Holy Spirit to lead me, and I began to study and seek more understanding using what I experienced with my mother as the foundation. I spoke with several hospice nurses, heard the testimonies of others who have been at the bedside of the dying, and studied everything I could. I learned of many similar experiences that confirmed the spiritual aspect of the dying process that I witnessed.

Although there are many books written about the physical process of dying, I found little written about the spiritual nature of dying from a biblical Judeo-Christian viewpoint or about how to use traditional biblical rituals during the dying process.

These lacks are what led me to write this book. I felt a strong calling from the Holy Spirit to write a guide for others to make them aware of and teach them about the spiritual aspect of the dying process and the established spiritual rituals that can be used to create a spiritual atmosphere of peace and love for those who are dying. I kept hearing the Spirit say, "People are dying. People need to know this." This kept me motivated.

After hundreds of hours of intense study, prayer, building upon over thirty-five years of biblical study and teachings concerning various aspects of Heaven, many shed tears as I re-lived my mother's final days numerous times, and the inspiration of the Holy Spirit, I have written this guidebook to expound on the spiritual aspect of dying that I discovered during my mother's death and what I have learned since.

End-of-Life Spiritual Care: Spiritual Insights and Biblical Rituals to Help Your Loved One Step into Eternity with Faith,

Love, and Dignity (End-of-Life Spiritual Care), is written from a Bible-based viewpoint. It illuminates the spiritual aspect of dying and what can be expected throughout the process. It also shares established biblical rituals with no specific denomination in mind to convey the godly spiritual principles that will create a sacred atmosphere to usher in the presence of the Holy Spirit to help those who are finishing the last chapter of their Book of Life on this Earth.

My purpose in writing this book is to help all people understand the spiritual aspect of the dying process to help their loved one step into eternity in as loving, hopeful, and dignified of a way as possible, as well as bless their own experience and memory of it. It is also to bring comfort to those who are going through the grieving process.

Blessings to you - the one, or family - who are ministering to your loved one at the end of their life. May the Spirit of the Lord and His angels be with you throughout this life-changing event. May you and your family be comforted and assured throughout the process. My heart and spirit are with you.

Rose Martin
January 3, 2023
Bella Vista, Arkansas

Introduction to
End-of-Life Spiritual Care

We enter the world alone and we leave the world alone. Dying is a journey each person must ultimately make on their own when it is their time. Even so, people want and need their family and friends with them to help them make the transition.

Over the next several years, many people will be making their transition from their earthly life to their heavenly life. You most likely know or will know someone whose time it is to make their journey.

While you will not be able to help heal the physical sickness of your loved one at the end of their life, you can help them as they prepare their soul and spirit to make their ultimate step into eternity. At this closing time in someone's life, you have the opportunity to help them complete it in a most peaceful way.

The transition of leaving our earthly life to go to our heavenly dwelling is something we all will go through, yet most of us do not think about it until the death of a loved one or at the time of our own death. Then it can be a frightening ordeal for both the dying and their family when they must deal with matters they have never even thought about before.

Taking the Mystery out of Dying

End-of-Life Spiritual Care: Spiritual Insights and Biblical Rituals to Help Your Loved One Step into Eternity with Faith, Love, and Dignity (End-of-Life Spiritual Care) takes some of the mystery out of dying by supplying factual insight into the end-of-life process that has not been freely shared before.

Its purpose is to make people aware of the spiritual aspects of dying and the marvel of what is happening through that process, some of which they may not see with their eyes but will feel with their hearts. It is written for everyday people who want to help their very special loved one step into eternity.

You Can Help Your Loved One

How can you help your loved one make their transition to eternity? Thankfully, the Spirit helps everyone through this process, but knowing more about it is very helpful for all that are involved.

The primary way you can be a support and comfort to your dying loved one is by simply being present and holding their hand without having to say a word (unless they want to talk of course!) and let them know that someone is with them. Going through the process of dying alone is hard. Having your company is very important.

In addition, you can help your loved one by providing a safe, faith-filled, loving, and spiritual environment that will enable them to do their work of dying in the most meaningful way possible. You can create a sacred space for them from which they can take their ultimate step out of this earthly life into their next phase of eternity.

Focusing on Spiritual Care

Spiritual care at the end of life is vital. At a time when there is nothing left to do medically, the spiritual should be the primary focus.

In most cases spiritual belief in Someone greater than themselves helps most people get past any darkness, fear, and loneliness they may experience and replace it with hope and direction for their journey. Providing spiritual protection and guidance are key factors in achieving peace at this time.

While books are available on the complete process of dying and supplying physical comfort, *End-of-Life Spiritual Care* focuses on providing spiritual comfort and support throughout the process. It highlights common spiritual items, rituals, and customs typically used throughout Bible-based faith that can easily be used to create a sacred atmosphere for the end-of-life work to be done.

PART ONE provides insight into the spiritual aspect of the labor of dying that your loved one is going through and how you can support them during the process. It also helps those who are grieving the loss of a loved one that has already passed on to grasp more understanding of eternal life and the amazing process that their loved one went through.

PART TWO prepares you or the one who will minister, the items you will use in the End-of-Life Ceremony (which is covered in later chapters), and the room itself before ministering to your loved one.

PART THREE brings common spiritual biblical rituals and customs into view and provides you with instructions and step-by-step examples on how to organize and perform an End-of-Life Ceremony. Using the familiar items found throughout Scripture you can create an atmosphere to build faith and bring peace, assurance, and strength to your loved one who is making this transition. This also helps to bring closure to your loved one's spouse, partner, children, family, friends, or caregivers who are with them as they make their journey to the other side.

PART FOUR includes a variety of Prayers, Scripture, and practical matters to help build faith, bring comfort, and organize your time at hospice while sitting vigil.

PART FIVE clarifies the spiritual viewpoint of this book and provides more information about the author and the background that supported the writing this book.

End-of-Life Spiritual Care is a complete guide to preparing a sacred space for your loved one at the end of their life and caring for them using the spiritual support that God provides for His children at this pivotal time of their life. You do not need to be a licensed minister to provide this care.

The acts of faith shared by you and your loved one through participating in the End-of-Life Ceremony will add to the significance of this special time. These final prayers and blessings will give your loved one spiritual comfort and renewed faith as they make their journey beyond the veil that separates life from death.

End-of-Life Spiritual Care will also be of value to anyone whose loved one has recently passed. It will give them comfort and clarity about the dying process their loved one experienced, where they are now, and that they are safe. Questions they have had about their loved one's death can be answered.

Personalize Your Use of Each Item

I encourage you to use *End-of-Life Spiritual Care* as a guide to plan and perform your own rituals, ceremonies, and prayers. With the Spirit's leading, use these articles according to your faith, denomination, spiritual beliefs, culture, or family customs to invoke the sacred aspect of the dying process during the final days of your loved one's life on this Earth. They will help bring stability and grace to this extremely emotional time.

Share Your Experience

When you are ready to share, it would be an honor to learn about your loved one's transition to eternity. Help encourage others who are going through this by letting them know of any guidance and comfort that this book provided in helping you during your loved one's dying process.

Let others know by posting an online review to share your experience. Or you can send it to us at:

SpiritualCareCollection@gmail.com where we may add it to the testimony page of www.End-of-Life-Spiritual-Care.com.

People who are making

their transition from

Earth to Heaven look for peace

and connection to God.

Many who are not necessarily

religious still express the desire

for spiritual support.

PART ONE

~ 1 ~

Dying is a Natural Spiritual Process

"...(God) has also set eternity in the hearts of men..."
Ecclesiastes 3:11

While it is true, Believers have been taught, "absent from the body, present with the Lord," there is a process that leads to this point that is not well understood or even talked about, but it is well known by those who care for the dying.

Dying involves the entire person - body, soul, and spirit. It is a natural process by which the soul and spirit separate from the body. It includes a life review. Setting an atmosphere that surrounds the dying person with peace and safety during this time of transition is important in supporting the separation and review that is taking place.

It is sown a natural body; it is raised a spiritual body.
If there is a natural body, there is also a spiritual body.
1 Corinthians 15:44 ESV

The Miracle of Birth and Death

The dying process is very much like the birthing process. Each one has recognizable stages of labor yet each one is unique. Each one leads to the beginning of a new life. Each one needs coaching and support. No two births or two deaths happen exactly the same way.

Participating in the birth of a baby is a wonder. Birth is a life-changing event as a soul, sent by God who created it, begins its new life on Earth. The baby's first breath signifies its passage to this world.

> *"Before I formed you in the womb I knew you,*
> *and before you were born I set you apart…"*
> *Jeremiah 1:5 BSB*
>
> *Your eyes saw my unformed body; all my days were*
> *written in Your book and ordained for me*
> *before one of them came to be. Psalm 139:16 BSB*
>
> *The Spirit of God has made me, and the breath of*
> *the Almighty gives me life. Job 33:4 BSB*

The death of an individual is a wonder too. It is a life-changing event as the soul and spirit leave the body to return to the God who created them. Death is the final act of living. The last breath here signifies the passage from this world to the next. Death is a spiritual event.

> *"I came from the Father and have come into the world,*
> *and now I am leaving the world and going*
> *to the Father." John 16:28 ESV*

Participating in the end of someone's life is also a wonder and a life-changing event. Those who have been at the bedside during the dying process can attest to Heaven's windows opening and supernatural love filling the air. There is an increase of faith, hope, and love and a presence of peace and joy which is noticeably experienced by the dying and their loved ones as death draws near, and at the time of death. To be involved in this process of a person's passing is an honor and a privilege.

While death is a powerful natural event, it can also be filled with fear, anxiety, and pain. Some typical concerns the dying have are:

- ♥ They do not want to leave their life on Earth.
- ♥ They do not want to leave their loved ones.
- ♥ They do not know where they are going, or what kind of place it will be.
- ♥ They do not know if the loved ones they are leaving will be alright.
- ♥ They experience the fear of the unknown.
- ♥ They may have unresolved issues that need to be worked out before they depart.

Everyone's Faith is Tested

During the ending of a life, everyone's faith is tested. We search for answers. In our search for answers, we are forced to think about the matters of life and death we normally do not think about.

- ♥ What is happening to our loved one?
- ♥ Where are they going?
- ♥ Will they be all right?

We are faced with questions about what we believe.

- ♥ In Whom do we believe?
- ♥ In what do we have our faith?
- ♥ What is life all about?

Both the actively dying and their loved ones need direction and assurance as to what is happening at this time.

The memories of the holidays we celebrated in our childhood, the religious teachings we received as youths, and the practice and growth of our faith as adults can reawaken and strengthen our faith and begin to set a foundation for this process. These remind us of the promise of eternal life and of a loving God.

Direction and Assurance

The articles of faith and celebrations typically found in biblical faith can give the spiritual direction and assurance needed in a non-denominational way. Performing traditional spiritual acts and rituals during the transition builds faith and trust in the process. These common spiritual rituals can create meaningful and beautiful memories. They can:

- ♥ Help neutralize fears.
- ♥ Provide the comfort, direction, and promise needed by everyone involved.
- ♥ Help individuals deal with the issues of their life that need to be settled before death.
- ♥ Create an environment favorable to take care of any unfinished business or mend any relationships with others that need to be reconciled.
- ♥ Help make the spiritual real.

Spiritual Symbols and Acts of Faith

There are widespread spiritual symbols and acts of faith that have been shared among many cultures and religions throughout history. They include:

- ♥ Sensitive and proper use of prayers
- ♥ Laying on of hands
- ♥ Purification (water)
- ♥ Anointing with oil
- ♥ Covering the head with a prayer shawl or scarf
- ♥ Partaking of bread and wine in communion
- ♥ Reading and proclaiming God's Word of restoration and life

These can be used to usher in a holy space in which a peaceful transition can take place. These symbols and rituals help us connect to the spiritual.

Faith Based Rituals

Faith-based rituals provide conduits for the dying to connect with the spiritual for support until the spiritual reality of what is happening is revealed to them. At that time, they will find the Light in the darkness themselves, where they know that they will be safe.

These practices help everyone to look to Someone or something greater than themselves for a safe journey. They remind us that our spirit and soul are eternal and that one day we too will be going 'home.' Most importantly, they help fulfill the final spiritual needs of the dying person during this transitional time of their life.

Life Review

During the dying process everyone goes through a life review, where "your whole life flashes before your eyes." Each person goes through a process in which every part of the life they have lived is reviewed. The veil begins to lift, and their life and purpose begin to be seen more clearly. Their own judgment of their life begins to take place.

In their life review, the dying are shown the truth, both good and bad, about the situations they have experienced in their lives and why they happened. They see how they have blessed or hurt people from the other person's perspective. They realize the effects of the words they have spoken. A chance for any forgiveness that is needed is also given before leaving.

The speed at which this happens is unique to each person. The review can take place in just the hours or minutes before death, through episodes that have played out over the months, weeks, or days leading up to it, or even after it in the case of a sudden death.

While there are joyous revelations, certain parts of the life review can be a challenge. Having a sacred environment to do this work provides stability.

> *For now we see in a mirror dimly, but then face to face.*
> *Now I know in part; then I shall know fully, even as*
> *I have been fully known.1 Corinthians 13:12 ESV*

> *...And just as it is appointed for man to die once, and*
> *after that comes judgment... Hebrews 9:27 ESV*

> *"But I tell you that men will give an account on the day*
> *of judgment for every careless word they have spoken.*
> *For by your words you will be acquitted, and by your*
> *words you will be condemned." Matthew 12:36-37 BSB*

Forgiveness and Love

One of the most significant spiritual needs of the dying is forgiveness – for themselves and others. The other is love. These two actions are particularly important both when we are alive and especially when we are dying. It is important to forgive and find reconciliation where necessary and whenever possible.

During your loved one's life review they may remember someone they hurt that they never apologized to, or they may remember someone that hurt them that they never forgave. This is the time for them to make amends and forgive any offenses. If they cannot see them in person, they can forgive them in the Spirit through prayer.

"And when you stand praying, if you hold anything against anyone, forgive them, so that your Father in heaven may forgive you your sins." Mark 11:25 NIV

'Love your neighbor as yourself.' There is no commandment greater than these." Mark 12:31 NIV

It is important to make peace if we can with everyone we have strife with before we die. Thankfully, there is more love available during the dying process to help make this possible. Love makes all things possible.

Saying Goodbye

Another need is to say goodbye and tell friends and relatives that they love them and perhaps recall special times they shared together. They need to know their family will be taken care of. They may need permission from their loved ones to die. It is the time to close the chapter 'here' as they prepare to go 'there.'

Now this is the blessing with which Moses the man of God blessed the sons of Israel before his death.
Deuteronomy 33:1 NAS

"Peace I leave with you; my peace I give you. I do not give to you as the world gives. Do not let your hearts be troubled and do not be afraid." John 14:27 NIV

Remembering Your Creator

The most important fulfilment of spiritual needs that can occur during the dying process is the union, or reunion and reconciliation, of a human being with their Creator - God. This is a most significant event.

Remember your Creator. Remember Him before the silver cord is snapped and the golden bowl is crushed...before the dust returns to the ground from which it came and the spirit returns to God who gave it.
Ecclesiastes 12:1, 6-7 BSB

Providing spiritual support is hugely beneficial in helping people find the Light of God, their Creator before that time. Spiritual rituals and ceremonies bring faith, respect, and love to the final days of one's life. They invite the presence of The Almighty God so they can rest in His arms of love. They can let go of their fear and find the courage to face this unknown.

God Ultimately Takes Over

The process of dying is as natural as the process of being born. We can make it as comfortable as possible, but we need to know that in the end God ultimately takes over and safely brings each one of His children home to a 'mansion' prepared especially for them. Spiritual ceremonies and rituals make the transition to Heaven meaningful for all. These actions and words bring significance to the final days of your loved one's life and spiritual growth for all involved.

For we know that if the tent that is our earthly home is
destroyed, we have a building from God, a house not
made with hands, eternal in the heavens.
2 Corinthians 5:1 ESV

You Do Not Need to be a Licensed Minister

Tending to the spiritual needs at the bedside of your loved one who is making their final journey home does not require you to be a licensed minister. With the love for God, a pure heart, and the right intentions, you can call on the Holy Spirit and God will activate the power and meaning of these rituals, bringing a blessing for the dying as well as for those present.

And whatever you do, whether in word or deed, do it all
in the name of the Lord Jesus, giving thanks to God the
Father through him. Colossians 3:17 NIV

To die peacefully can be a glorious event, although this is not always the case. Thankfully, the efforts of caring people can help many make a peaceful transition. Each person involved has a unique quality, a gift, that only they can give to the one who is dying.

A Spiritual Awakening

Death is a mysterious, powerful event for all involved. It is a reminder that our life on Earth is temporary and the importance of living it to the fullest while we are here. The death process can build unity among those present as they share this life-changing event together. Most everyone involved with those who are dying experiences a spiritual awakening of some sort during the process.

You can help your loved one make their transition to Heaven. In addition to spending your time with them, you can offer the symbols of faith typically associated with the spiritual aspects of life and death. They can create a holy atmosphere to help your loved one work through the remaining issues of life that need to be addressed before they cross over. PART TWO will begin to explain what these special items of faith are and how to use them.

When the Silver Cord is Broken

When your loved one has finished their time on earth and the 'silver cord' is broken (Ecclesiastes 12:6), they will be with the Lord, being ministered to by angels and their loved ones that have gone before. They will meet with the Heavenly Council and Elders to further review their lives and future. Until that time, there is a lot of work to be done to finish their time on Earth while they are still in the physical. Providing a spirit-filled atmosphere that honors God and the person who is dying will greatly aid in this life-altering process.

So we are always of good courage. We know that while we are at home in the body we are away from the Lord, for we walk by faith, not by sight. Yes, we are of good courage, and we would rather be away from the body and at home with the Lord. So whether we are at home or away, we make it our aim to please him. For we must all appear before the judgment seat of Christ, so that each one may receive what is due for what he has done in the body, whether good or evil.
2 Corinthians 5:6-10 ESV

And he said, "Jesus, remember me when you come into your kingdom." And he said to him, "Truly, I say to you, today you will be with me in paradise."
Luke 23:42-43 ESV

PART TWO

~ 2 ~
Setting the Spiritual Atmosphere

People who are making their transition from Earth to Heaven look for peace and connection to God. Many who are not necessarily religious still express the desire for spiritual support.

When the spirit and soul are ready to go 'home' there is a common spirituality that goes beyond denominations. The experience of life and death are shared by all, and it unites us all, regardless of spiritual beliefs, doctrines, or monetary status.

Spirituality is reflected in symbols and rituals that many people, cultures, religions, and societies recognize for their deeper eternal and often mysterious meanings. These become increasingly important at the end of life.

Inviting the Holy Spirit

Through rituals and customs, inviting the Holy Spirit, and ushering in an atmosphere of love, you can create a holy space in which your loved one can make a peaceful transition to eternity with love and dignity. It will help everyone to say goodbye.

Invoking the sacred will create a holy atmosphere that will allow your loved one's spirit and soul to separate from their physical body more easily when it is time for them to go. It will not speed up the dying process, but it will help calm any fears they have of leaving and give them the assurance and confidence to let go.

Being Sensitive to Your Loved One's Beliefs

Throughout this process it is important to be sensitive to the spiritual beliefs and requests of the dying. Remember to take care of their spiritual needs first and not yours. Not everyone will accept spiritual help.

Important: When performing these rituals, or any other activity, guard against getting too emotional as your loved one may get overwhelmed or overstimulated and may not be able to express it. Keep watch to see how your loved one is doing throughout all your activities.

Hospice Nurse Mary Beth Willi, LPN, author of, *Learning to Let Go The Signs and Symptoms of the Dying Process*, shared with me from her many years of experience in dealing with end-of-life care some of the reasons the dying may become agitated when offering spiritual help:

"If your loved one is unable to speak, you will know if something upsets them if they become agitated or restless.

"The one thing I would recommend is to be careful with the strings attached to God's love or getting into Heaven, especially at the end of life. It can really upset them.

"Some are mad at God and don't want to hear anything about Him. There are a lot of religious people who are angry at God for one reason or another.

"People need to know that in the dying process all the rules can go right out the window.

"What we witnessed was, 'Whether you believe in God or not, He believes in you.'

"If you feel strongly about them accepting Jesus Christ as their Savior and being born again, you can think it and you can pray for them. I did A LOT of praying for peace. Just don't say it out loud to them.

"You have to meet them where they are. A lot of them eventually talked about God. But we sometimes had to wait for them to do that first.

"If the family is worried about the patient not being saved, I would tell them… *'You have no idea of what is in their heart. Just wait until their life review is finished and you may see them 'go back to God.'*

"And if they didn't get to witness that I would remind them… *'You have no idea of what is in their heart. You shouldn't judge another person.'*

"I knew God was taking them home and I tried my best to get them to understand that."

Prayer for Salvation

With the previous guidance in mind, depending on your loved one's spiritual state, you can reaffirm or introduce them to faith in Yeshua as Savior. You can tell them about His love and ask them if they want to put their trust in Him to bring them safely to the other side.

If your loved one wishes to accept or reaffirm Yeshua as their Savior, ask them to repeat after you as you read each sentence.

Prayer:

> "Lord Jesus, Come into my life."
> "I believe in You and the sacrifice You made on the Tree of Sacrifice for me."
> "I believe you shed Your blood, died, were buried, and rose again from the grave and that You live eternally in Heaven."
> "Forgive me of all my sins."
> "Cleanse me from all unrighteousness."
> "Move into my heart."
> "I make You my Lord and Savior."
> "I accept Your free gift of eternal life."
> "I look forward to meeting You face to face."
> "Thank You Lord. So be it."

When someone only has the strength to speak a few words simply saying, "Jesus, please save me," from the heart is all that is needed.

Like angels waiting for you to ask them for help, God waits for everyone to ask Him to come into their life. Ask and He will open the door for you.

> *Behold, I stand at the door and knock. If anyone hears my voice and opens the door, I will come in to him and eat with him, and he with me. Revelation 3:20 ESV*

*Then he brought them out and asked, "Sirs, what must I
do to be saved?" They replied, "Believe in the Lord Jesus
and you will be saved, you and your household."*
Acts 16:30-31 NIV

*This is good, and it is pleasing in the sight of God our
Savior, who desires all people to be saved and to come to
the knowledge of the truth. For there is one God, and
there is one mediator between God and men, the man
Christ Jesus, who gave himself as a ransom for all, which
is the testimony given at the proper time.*
1 Timothy 2:3-6 ESV

Ask God to Send His Holy Spirit

Ask God to come into the space where one of His children is preparing to come home and He will send the Holy Spirit, the angels, even loved ones who are already there to guide, to protect, and welcome your loved one as the doors of Heaven are being opened. Believe in the power of God. Believe that God is GOD.

Call in God's help through the Holy Spirit, also referred to as the Comforter, as well as His angels when extra support is needed. They will come in response to your calls.

The Sense of Hearing is the Last to Go

Be aware that hearing is generally the last sense to go when dying. Even if your loved is unresponsive, they most likely hear everything that is going on in the room. You can purposely hold family conversations, share memories, and include your loved one even if they do not respond. They might also enjoy just listening to your voices as you have conversations with each other!

In the same way, as you prepare to perform these rituals, everything you say and do to create this sacred space will be heard not only by God, the Holy Spirit, and the angels, but by your loved one! They will hear you.

You give your loved one a powerful gift when you prepare a sacred space, anoint, and bless them. These spiritual acts will help give them peace and direction for their journey.

Each death will unfold differently but you now have a foundation on which to get started. Like the birth process, each death is unique. As with birth, it is a life-changing experience for all involved.

~ 3 ~
End-of-Life Ceremony Outline

The following outline lists the components that make up the rituals that can be used to create a ceremony that will help prepare a sacred space for your loved one.

The End-of-Life Ceremony begins by preparing the person who will perform, or minister, the rituals. They will prepare themselves, the items they will be using, and the room.

Once everything has been prepared, they and their family will focus their loving attention on the ceremonial purifying and anointing of their loved one, adorning them with a prayer shawl, taking part in communion as a family, followed by family fellowship, and sealing it with the Aaronic Blessing.

Quick Reference Guide

Below is the quick reference list of the items that are described in *End-of-Life Spiritual Care* that can be used in your personalized spiritual End-of-Life Ceremony.

The order of how they are listed is an example of the order in which an End-of-Life Ceremony can be conducted and celebrated with friends and family, or individually with your loved one. The pages referenced lead straight to the examples and prayers for quick access if needed.

| END-OF-LIFE CEREMONY - QUICK REFERENCE GUIDE ||
CEREMONY COMPONENT	PAGE
Setting the Spiritual Atmosphere	23
Setting Apart the Special Items	31
Preparing the One Who Will Minister	35
Anointing the Room	39
Lighting the Candle	41
Beginning the End-of-Life Ceremony	43
Praying Over the Sacred Time	44
Purifying Your Loved One with Water	51
Anointing Your Loved One with Oil	55
Ministering the Anointing	61
Adorning the Prayer Shawl or Scarf	68
Officiating the Last Supper	73
Sealing with the Aaronic Blessing	77
Daily Spiritual Care	81
If Death is Delaying	85
At the Actual Death	89
Sudden Death	95

These components are described in more detail in the following chapters.

Important: When performing these rituals, or any other activity, guard against getting too emotional as your loved one may get overwhelmed or overstimulated and may not be able to express it. Monitor them and observe how they are doing throughout all your activities.

If your loved one is unable to speak, you will know if something upsets them if they become agitated or restless.

~ 4 ~
Special Items for End-of-Life Rituals

The items introduced here are traditional spiritual elements referenced throughout the Bible. They are commonly used to invite the presence of the Heavenly Hosts and create a sacred environment for God's presence to dwell. They can be used during the sacred time leading up to death to comfort, protect, and guide you throughout the experience.

> *"And let them make me a sanctuary,*
> *that I may dwell in their midst." Exodus 25:8*

Seek the Holy Spirit as to which items you are to include, the prayers you are to pray, when and how to use them, and then use them in the way you are led.

I have included examples on how to implement each component of the spiritual rituals. Please individualize them for your specific situation.

Items that Welcome the Holy Spirit

These are the items that are typically used to welcome the Holy Spirit of God and prepare a comforting atmosphere. Use them simply or lavishly or anywhere in between as you are led.

- ♥ Prayer
- ♥ Candle
- ♥ Bowl of Pure Water
- ♥ Anointing Oil
- ♥ Prayer Shawl
- ♥ Bread and Grape Juice for Communion
- ♥ Saying Prayers and Reading Scriptures

The biblical and spiritual meaning of these items are described in the following chapters along with examples of how to use them. The examples are guidelines of how to implement these items. They can be adapted and personalized to fulfill the preferences of various biblical interpretations and Christian denominations. You can add to or change them to tailor them to fit your customs, traditions, and needs as your situation calls for and as the Spirit leads. These items will set the spiritual tone for the entire process.

You can perform all these rituals throughout one visit or use each one at separate times. Take as long as you would like with each one or go through them quickly if that is what is called for. Each situation will be different.

Thereafter, daily prayer while sitting at the bedside of your loved one and spending time in Scripture will keep the presence of Spirit of God in the atmosphere. Standard prayers like "The Lord's Prayer" and for Catholics adding the "Hail Mary" recited daily can help strengthen and focus everyone's faith for what that day will bring.

Catholic Guideline

From CATHOLIC GUIDELINES FOR THE DYING: These acts can be used as part of the Last Sacraments in the Catholic Church and are typically performed by a priest. If a priest is not available, they can be administered by a loved one or another minister. The Last Rites of the Catholic Church are Confession, Anointing, and Holy Communion.

You can perform all these rituals throughout one visit or use each one at separate times.

Take as long as you would like with each one or go through them quickly if that is what is called for.

Each situation will be different.

~ 5 ~
Cleansing the Spiritual Atmosphere

Preparing Yourself and the Sacred Items

Preparing the spiritual atmosphere begins with the spiritual purifying of everything involved with this sacred time. To start, the one who will be performing the unction should prepare themselves.

> Unction: Welcoming Holy Spirit power through the anointing of oil; the anointing with oil by the pouring of oil on an item or body part to release the power of the Holy Spirit.

As the one who will minister, you are going to spiritually purify yourself first and then sanctify the room and everything you will be using. This is to clear away anything that is not of God's Spirit to provide a pure atmosphere to make way for the Holy things of God.

> *'Prepare the way for the Lord, make straight paths for Him.' Mark 1:3 BSB*

Begin with a Prayer

Pray to God in the Name of Yeshua. Set your focus on what you are going to do and why you are doing it. Ask to be cleansed of any impurity. Ask for the Holy Spirit to guide and direct this process. Pray for the best and highest outcome for all involved.

Prayer:

"Lord, cleanse me and prepare me for this holy time together with our loved one. Search my heart for any sin. Forgive me and remove any impurity. Use me as a vessel for Your love to flow through. I ask for the Holy Spirit to guide me as I minister to our loved one."

Bless the Articles

Pray over all the articles you will be using. Gather the bowl and water, anointing oil, candle, shawl or scarf, and communion items – set them apart spiritually for holy use during this sacred time.

Prayer:

"Lord, I ask that You purify these articles through the blood of Yeshua (Life is in the blood) and the light of God. Make them instruments of Your Holiness to bring peace and comfort to our loved one."

Purify Yourself with Water

Cleanse yourself symbolically with the water and pray.

Example:

Touch the fingers of your right hand into the bowl of water then, with those wet fingers, touch your forehead, the top of your head, the back of your neck, your heart, your right and then left palm, and finally, at the point where the toes meet the foot, your right and then left foot.

Prayer:

"In the Name of Yeshua, cleanse me of anything that is impure and make me a vessel for Your love and peace. Prepare me to minister to our loved one."

Anoint Yourself with Oil

In a similar pattern as used when purifying with water, put the oil on your right thumb and anoint yourself with oil while praying.

Prayer:

In the Name of the Father, Son, and Holy Spirit, I ask that You, God Almighty, anoint and equip me to minister to our loved one today. Lead me in Your highest and best way for all as we share this sacred time together.

Now you are ready to prepare the spiritual atmosphere of the room and those in it.

As the one who will minister, you

are going to spiritually

purify yourself first

and then sanctify the room

and everything you will be using.

This is to clear away anything that

is not of God's Spirit to provide

a pure atmosphere to make way

~ 6 ~

Anointing Your Loved One's Room

Purify and Set Apart the Room with Water and Oil

To anoint for spiritual purposes means to smear or rub oil or perfume on an individual or an object to set them apart for divine use. In this case, we want to set apart, make holy, the room of your loved one and everyone in it for the holy work of dying.

> *"Then you shall take the anointing oil and anoint the tabernacle and everything that is in it, and consecrate it and all its furnishings; and it shall be holy."*
> *Exodus 40:9 NAS*

Anointing oil is a symbol of faith in God and of His ability to cleanse and make things holy. There is nothing magical about the oil itself, even though it is a powerful tool of faith. As with all other spiritual tools, they are only a symbol. The real power comes from God.

Lift up your heads, you gates, And be lifted up,
you ancient doors, That the King of glory may come in!
Who is the King of glory? The LORD strong and mighty,
The LORD mighty in battle. Psalm 24:8-9 NAS

Anoint the room and every item and person in it with water or
oil or both. If there is medical equipment in the room, you can
cover it with sheets to make the room more relaxed. If there is
a roommate, you can hang a sheet, if possible, between the beds
to create privacy.

Place the anointing oil on each of the doors and frames,
windows, the bed, and other places and objects throughout the
entire room, as led. Anoint the forehead of the friends and
family that are present.

Example:

To anoint, place a dab of oil onto your right thumb and touch
each item you want to include with the oil. As you are
anointing the room, pray according to your beliefs.

Prayer:

"In the Name of Yeshua, we cleanse and purify this room
and everyone and everything in it. We bring everything into
submission to the mighty Name of Yeshua. We command all
disruptive, lingering spirits to be gone, we cast out fear and
invite the Holy Spirit and God's Holy angels to fill this room
with His love and peace during this momentous time in our
loved one's life."

"Mighty God, fill this space with Your Holy Spirit so that
everything that happens here will be done in accordance with
Your will. Turn this place where we are standing into Holy
ground for Your Holy use."

Now the room and everything in it has been purified and
anointed, set apart, holy, ready for the spiritual work to be done.

~ 7 ~
Lighting the Candle

Candlelight provides a calming atmosphere, an ambiance that is soothing, healing, and helps ease and soften the mind. Candles are used around the world in various faiths and cultures and play a significant role in end-of-life rituals. Candles are used both during life and death.

Important: The use of battery-operated candles is highly recommended if oxygen is being used in the room. Oxygen is highly flammable, and the small flame of a candle can ignite it! Do not leave lit candles unattended. Use safety precautions with any open flame.

Significant Characteristics of the Candle

Lighting a candle is a ritual that promotes reflection and signifies a special time. It can bring hidden things to light.

Lighting the candle with spiritual intention alerts the heavenly hosts that you are asking for attention and help. It will create an atmosphere of spiritual support.

The candle is a reminder of the eternal spark or the flame of life that is within each person. It illustrates the transition from material – the wax and the wick, to spirit – the flame.

The Christian faith believes the lighting of a candle symbolizes the Light of Christ.

Then Jesus again spoke to them, saying, "I am the Light of the world; the one who follows Me will not walk in the darkness, but will have the Light of life."
John 8:12 NAS

Lighting and displaying the candle is seen as an act of faith in Christ and being prepared to meet Him.

"Be dressed ready for service and keep your lamps burning, like servants waiting for their master to return from a wedding banquet, so that when he comes and knocks they can immediately open the door for him."
Luke 12:35-36 NIV

Example:

Place the candle at the bedside along with other pictures or cherished items and pray as you light it.

Prayer:

"Gracious and loving God, as I light this candle, I remember Your light which shines in the darkness. I ask that Your light fills this room through Your presence. I ask that Your Son, whose life, death, and resurrection gives us hope, be the Light guiding for our loved one at this time. I welcome Your Spirit which fills every corner of our lives."

PART THREE

~ 8 ~
Beginning the End-of-Life Ceremony

Turn Your Attention to Your Loved One

After you have purified yourself and any others, the articles to be used, the room, and lit the candle, it is now time to focus on your loved one. They are bringing to an end the final chapter of their time on this Earth. They are getting ready to move to the next part of their journey, to the spiritual heavenly side.

PLEASE NOTE: As you begin this loving time together, it is important to keep watch and monitor how your loved one is doing throughout all your activities.

Guard against getting too emotional as your loved one may become overwhelmed or overstimulated and may not be able to express it.

If your loved one is unable to speak, you will know if something upsets them if they become agitated or restless. At some point they may settle down in their life review and that may be a good time when you can try again.

Pray Over This Sacred Time

Begin your ceremony time together with a prayer to fill the cleansed space. The prayers create a container or holder for the entire event. Your ending prayer will seal your time together as it is recorded in the Heavenly records.

Ask that your loved one be ministered to throughout the process you will be facilitating. Ask for the Holy Spirit and the angels to help prepare your loved one to receive the love of God during this time. Ask for this time together to serve the highest good for your loved one and all that are concerned.

Prayer:

"Lord, we come together in Your Name to help our loved one make their journey home to You. Holy Spirit, You are welcomed in this place. We have cleansed and purified our hearts and minds, the items we will be using, and the room to make a place for You to dwell during this entire process. Direct, guide, and bless our time together."

"We pray for You God, the Holy Spirit, the angels, to be with our loved one and guide them through this transition. Help them to get ready to go to the place that You have prepared for them. Forgive their sins and show them Your Love. May they be welcomed by their friends and relatives that have gone before."

"At this time, we ask that You make this room a place where our loved one can complete their work on this Earth and leave in peace, and that those who remain will find comfort in the realization that our loved one is in a safe place, in the arms of Love. In Yeshua's Name, so be it."

You can use the additional Prayers and Scriptures referenced throughout *End-of-Life Spiritual Care,* and in Chapters 22 through 25, or others that you find inspirational around which to build your prayers and declarations of faith.

Ask God to send His Holy

Spirit to cleanse your loved one

of any fear, doubt, anxiety,

worldly attachment,

or any other spiritual impurity

in the Name of Yeshua.

~ 9 ~
Preparing Your Loved One

Purifying with Water and Anointing with Oil

During the dying process, purifying and anointing your loved one cleanses them and sets them apart to do the labor of dying with the help of their Creator. It clears their connection to the Spirit of God during a time when they are getting their final affairs in order – their life review, making amends, saying goodbyes, saying hello to their new life.

In biblical teachings, the Holy Spirit, given to us by God, dwells in us. Our bodies are the temple of the Holy Spirit and should be honored and purified while making the transition.

> *Or do you not know that your body is a temple of the*
> *Holy Spirit within you, whom you have from God,*
> *and that you are not your own?*
> *1 Corinthians 6:19 NAS*

Treating the body with respect is part of dying with dignity. Cleansing and anointing are both physical and spiritual, as the soul and spirit are still connected to the body.

Water is the true symbol of purification. Not only do we use it to wash and clean our physical bodies, but we can also use it to cleanse our soul and spirit.

Traditional rituals include washing the face, hands, and feet of the one who is dying. This is something that can be done prior to this time of spiritual purification and anointing.

The Various Meanings of Baptism and Immersion

Spiritual purifying can be done at many times throughout a person's life. Some denominations will baptize at birth, at a baby dedication, some at the time of transition from childhood to adulthood, some at the time of salvation. It is done in preparation for the observance of special holy days on the biblical calendar or at any time cleansing is desired. It is also done when approaching death.

> ...let us draw near to God with a sincere heart and with
> the full assurance that faith brings, having our hearts
> sprinkled to cleanse us from a guilty conscience and
> having our bodies washed with pure water.
> Let us hold unswervingly to the hope we profess,
> for he who promised is faithful. Hebrews 10:22-23 NIV

In the Christian faith, after professing faith in Yeshua ha Mashiach, the Lord Jesus Christ, as their Savior, gentiles go down into the water to signify leaving the old self behind. They die to their pagan ways and come out of the water as a newborn child, with a new identity, faith, and commitment. They are spiritually reborn. Baptism symbolizes that they are washed clean of sin and now have a new life.

> Therefore if anyone is in Christ, he is a new creation.
> The old has passed away. Behold, the new has come!
> 2 Corinthians 5:17 NIV

The immersion and coming out of the water also represent the death, burial, and resurrection of Christ. It stands for the death and dying of our natural selves and rising to new life of faith. It is like being born-again.

> *We were therefore buried with Him through baptism*
> *into death, in order that, just as Christ was raised from*
> *the dead through the glory of the Father,*
> *we too may walk in newness of life. Romans 6:4 ESV*

> *For as many of you as were baptized into Christ*
> *have put on Christ. Galatians 3:27 ESV*

Various denominations use a variety of methods of applying the water ranging from sprinkling to full body immersion. All have the same intention in mind – to reaffirm and proclaim faith in God and to wash away impurity.

At the time nearing death, it is also a symbol of being washed clean of all the earthly ties, ready to go to a new life in Heaven.

The Mikvah – The Waters of Purification

In the Jewish faith, worshippers become ritually clean before God in a full water immersion, called the Mikvah. The Mikvah is also called the 'waters of purification.' It is regarded as a pure, unadulterated avenue of connection with God. Mikvah for the Jews personifies both the womb and the grave, the portals to life and the afterlife. As such it is a place where hope is reawakened and strengthened.

In Hebrew, the same letters that spell the word Mikvah also spell 'hope.' The Messianic Jewish/Christian faith takes part regularly through immersion in the Mikvah.

The power and meaning of all these Scriptures, symbolisms, and practices come together at this time to bring hope and faith to all as you bless and purify your loved one with water in preparation for their new life.

~ 10 ~

Purifying Your Loved One by Sprinkling of Water

At the time nearing death, you can symbolically cleanse your loved one's body, soul, and spirit to prepare them for their journey home.

Ask God to send His Holy Spirit to cleanse your loved one of any fear, doubt, anxiety, worldly attachment, or any other spiritual impurity in the Name of Yeshua.

Example:

Take the bowl with water that you prepared earlier. Touch the fingers of your right hand into the bowl of water then, with those wet fingers, touch the middle of your loved one's forehead, the crown of their head, the back of their neck, their heart area, their right and then left palm (your left and their right), and then the right and left foot, at the point where their toes meet the foot. As you are applying the water, you can pray.

Prayer:

"Heavenly Father, Our Creator, the Living God, You created us and know us all. You are everywhere. We ask that You cleanse our loved one of all that is not of Love. Heal them, renew them, transform them during this time of transition."

"May Your healing water purify them so that Your Spirit and theirs can do their work. May love and kindness surround our loved one as they prepare to meet You. Wash away the things of Earth as they put on their heavenly garment."

I will sprinkle clean water on you, and you will be clean;
I will cleanse you from all your impurities
and from all your idols. Ezekiel 36:25 NIV

Water Baptism for Declaration of Faith

While we have been speaking of sprinkling or anointing with water to cleanse, if someone wishes to be water baptized in the Name of Yeshua, Jesus, this would be a good time to do it.

If your loved one is still responsive you can ask if they have been baptized in the Name of Yeshua as their Savior. If they have, Praise the Lord. If not, you can ask them if they would like to be baptized into the Name of Jesus and pray with them.

If your loved one is no longer responsive, you can ask others that are in close relationship to them, the family that is present, if they would agree for your loved one to be baptized now for the forgiveness of sins and to receive the Holy Spirit.

You can ask your loved one:

"Have you received Jesus Christ (Yeshua ha Mashiach) as your Lord and Savior?"
"Do you believe in Him and His Word?"
– Both Yes.

Then the following words can be spoken as you sprinkle them, or wet their head, whichever is most appropriate, with the water that has been blessed.

Prayer:

"Because you have professed your faith in the Lord Jesus, I baptize you in the Name of Jesus the Christ for the remission of sin. Receive the gift of the Holy Spirit."

(Sprinkle or immerse the head as appropriate.)

Peter replied, "Repent and be baptized, every one of you,
in the name of Jesus Christ for the forgiveness
of your sins, and you will receive
the gift of the Holy Spirit.
This promise belongs to you and your children
and to all who are far off—to all whom
the Lord our God will call to Himself."
Acts 2:38-39 ESV

Catholic Guideline

From CATHOLIC GUIDELINES FOR THE DYING: When someone faces a life-threatening condition, a priest should be called. If they are unbaptized, a priest may baptism them. If a priest is not available, anyone can baptize in danger of death by pouring clean water over the head and saying, "I baptize you in the name of the Father, and of the Son, and of the Holy Spirit." This should only be done if it is in accord with the desire of the sick person.

To die peacefully can be a glorious event,

although this is not always the case.

Thankfully, the efforts of caring people can

help many make a peaceful transition.

Each person involved has a unique quality,

a gift, that only they can give

to the one who is dying.

~ 11 ~

Setting Apart Your Loved One with Oil

Anointing with oil is a symbol of faith in God and of His ability to set apart and make things Holy. It represents the Holy Spirit coming upon us to heal, empower, and bless.

Is anyone among you sick? Let them call the elders of the church to pray over them and anoint them with oil in the name of the Lord. And the prayer offered in faith will make the sick person well... James 5:14-15 NIV

Anointing with oil is generally used for healing, but at the point of death it is more for sanctifying the body, making it ready for the transition.

Anointing Oil is a Symbol of God's Spirit

In the Old Testament anointing oil was not merely a tool in a ceremony. It foreshadowed the work of the Holy Spirit that was to come to dwell within us in New Testament times.

The oil represents the Holy Spirit, as oil was used to anoint spiritual leaders in the Bible and afterwards the Holy Spirit came upon them. It was originally used exclusively to anoint and set apart priests and the Tabernacle articles, but its use was later extended to kings.

> *Then he poured some of the anointing oil on Aaron's*
> *head and anointed him, to consecrate him.*
> *Leviticus 8:12 ESV*

> *Then Samuel took the horn of oil and anointed him in*
> *the midst of his brothers. And the Spirit of*
> *the LORD rushed upon David from that day forward.*
> *1 Samuel 16:13 ESV*

In the early New Testament Church new followers of Christ were 'chrismated,' anointed with oil after baptism, in a sacrament called Chrismation, where they received a share in the royal priesthood of Christ and were sealed with the Holy Spirit. They were to be witnesses to the Truth. Anointing with oil is meaningful and powerful.

Believers are Equipped to Anoint

Believers in Yeshua ha Mashiach, Jesus the Messiah, are kings and priests in God's heavenly kingdom and can therefore release the unction through anointing oil for spiritual purposes as well. Believers are equipped to anoint in the Name of Yeshua.

*"Very truly I tell you, whoever believes in me will do the
works I have been doing, and they will do even greater
things than these, because I am going to the Father."
John 14:12 NIV*

*But you are a chosen people, a royal priesthood, a holy
nation, God's special possession, that you may declare
the praises of him who called you out of darkness
into his wonderful light. 1 Peter 2:9 NIV*

Anointing Oil Helps to Let Go

The physical body has a very strong drive to continue to live
even when it cannot support the soul and spirit any longer. The
anointing process lets the physical body know that it is all right,
and it can safely let go and release the soul and spirit.

People who are facing death seek peace and connection to God.
The unction is a way to help people draw closer to God and the
spiritual realm, which will help them release from the earthly
realm.

The anointing breaks the yoke, the bondage, the obstacles, the
hold that life on Earth has on our lives. Burdens are removed
and destroyed because of the anointing.

*It shall come to pass in that day that his burden
will be taken away from your shoulder, and his yoke
from your neck, and the yoke will be destroyed
because of the anointing oil. Isaiah 10:47 NKJV*

Taking Away the Burdens

Yeshua takes away the burdens of this world. Faith in Yeshua
breaks the yoke, the tie to Earth. His yoke is easy. His burden

is light. When your loved one gives their burdens to the Lord, they can find rest for their soul and let go.

> *"Come to me, all who labor and are heavy laden,*
> *and I will give you rest. Take my yoke upon you,*
> *and learn from me, for I am gentle and lowly in heart,*
> *and you will find rest for your souls. For my yoke is*
> *easy, and my burden is light." Matthew 11:28-30 NIV*

Yeshua Was Anointed with Oil Before His Death

The woman who poured the expensive perfume on Yeshua's head and feet was anointing Him with oil. She was symbolically preparing Him for His death.

> *Mary therefore took a pound of expensive ointment*
> *made from pure nard, and anointed the feet of Jesus*
> *and wiped his feet with her hair. The house was*
> *filled with the fragrance of the perfume. John 12:3 ESV*

> *"By pouring this perfume on Me, she has prepared My*
> *body for burial. Truly I tell you, wherever this gospel is*
> *preached in all the world, what she has done will also be*
> *told in memory of her." Matthew 26:12-13 BSB*

Anointing is a Gift for All

Anointing someone who is in the dying process is a gift not only to them, but to all who are left behind, because anointing helps all parties let go. It helps the spirit and soul release from the physical form of our dying friend or family member. It helps us to be able to release our loved one from our physical world. It helps us let go of our emotional hold on them.

What Type of Oil to Use

You can use prepared bottled anointing oil, or other oils such as olive oil or special oil from Israel, or oil blessed by your loved one's Pastor, Priest, or Rabbi.

You can use scented oils such as lavender if the aroma does not bother those in the room or use unscented oil if there is a sensitivity to fragrance. The oil will have been blessed and set apart by you earlier during the preparation.

Even though unction is a powerful tool of faith, there is nothing supernatural about the oil itself. As with all other spiritual tools, the real power comes from God. When we anoint with oil and perform the unction, we are calling upon the power of God through His Holy Spirit to move in our lives.

When to Anoint

You can anoint your loved one with oil at any time but particularly when they are nearing death from sickness or natural causes. You do not need to wait until they are at the point of death to anoint them. However, at the point of death, and after, they can be anointed with oil again.

Anointing someone who is in the dying

process is a gift not only to them,

but to all who are left behind, because

anointing helps all parties let go.

It helps the spirit and soul release from

the physical form of our dying

friend or family member.

It helps us to be able to release our

loved one from our physical world.

It helps us let go of

our emotional hold on them.

~ 12 ~

Ministering the Anointing

You will be ministering to your loved one by anointing their body with oil. You can vary this ritual to make it work for your circumstances. Anointing all the points of the body is best, but if you don't have access to the entire body, you can anoint only the middle of the forehead, the crown of the head, the back of the neck, and the heart in the middle of the chest, or only the forehead alone.

Praying Before, During, and After

The mystery of the unction, the mystery of releasing Holy Spirit power through anointing with oil, includes praying before, during, and after applying the oil. This is the oil that was prepared earlier to use for holy purposes at this time.

Example:

While in a prayerful attitude, with sacred intent, place your right thumb or index finger into the oil and then anoint the middle of the forehead of your loved one in the shape of the Cross as you are saying,

Prayer:

"I anoint you in the Name of the Father, the Son, and the Holy Spirit. May God's grace be bestowed upon your spirit, soul, and body. May the power of the Holy Spirit be with you."

As you continue to pray, continue to apply a small amount of oil to the other parts of the body making the sign of the cross if you choose, on the eyes, nostrils, mouth, earlobes, the top of their head, back of their neck, their heart area, their right and then left palm, and finally, at the point where the toes meet the foot on their right and then left foot. Replenish the oil as needed.

Continue and repeat any of the following short prayers while anointing your loved one:

- ♥ *The seal of the Holy Spirit.*

- ♥ *May the power of the Holy Spirit be upon you.*

- ♥ *May the Lord bless you and keep you,*

- ♥ *May the Lord cause His favor to shine upon you and be gracious unto you,*

- ♥ *May the Lord lift His favor unto you and give you peace.*

- ♥ *May the 'Oil of joy' of the Lord purify your body, soul, and spirit.*

- ♥ *May the Holy Spirit set you apart and protect you.*

- ♥ *May your soul and spirit find rest.*

The mystery of the unction sets your loved one apart and forms a shield of God's protection around them.

Setting Apart the Whole Person

The areas of the body that are anointed with oil represent the areas of life that are being blessed by the Holy Spirit, sanctified, and set apart. Briefly, they are the:

Forehead – in the middle of the forehead, the pineal gland. Thoughts, spiritual insight, beliefs. The mind.

Top of the Head – the very top of the head, by the soft spot. The Crown of the head; the authority one is under. The point where the soul and spirit leave the body.

Earlobes – the bottom of the ears. Hearing the voice of God clearly.

Neck – the back of the neck. Carrying the weight, the pressure, of the world. Heavy burdens being lifted, breaking the yoke.

Heart – in the middle of the chest. Love, the soul and spirit, the energy that supports the physical body.

Palms of hands – the inside of the hands. The work that is done with the hands. Works and deeds.

Feet – the place where the toes meet the foot. The concentration of nerve endings that connect to the whole body. The path that is walked in life.

You can also anoint the right earlobe, right thumb, right foot big toe. The right side is considered the stronger, cleaner side of the body in the Bible.

> *"The priest shall then put some of the oil ... on the lobe of the right ear of the one to be cleansed, and on the thumb of his right hand and on the big toe of his right foot." Leviticus 14:28 NIV*

Here it refers to the cleansing of a priest of God to prepare him for his sacred work. In this instance, dying is the sacred work that is being done.

Right Earlobe – needed to listen to the voice of God and correctly hear His message. To hear the Word of God and follow it.

Right Thumb – needed to handle the things of God. To set apart for God everything they put their hands to - their deeds.

Right Big Toe of Foot – needed for balance. To walk righteously through the steps they take in life to fulfill their God-given purpose. To remember God in their faith-walk.

~ 13 ~
The Prayer Shawl and Scarf

He who dwells in the shelter of the Most High
will abide in the shadow of the Almighty. Psalm 91:1 ESV

Another form of protection and comfort is the prayer shawl. Nothing is better than to feel wrapped in God's love, safe in His arms, and covered by His grace, especially when death is approaching.

Physical and Spiritual Comfort

A prayer shawl or scarf offers comfort to the dying, both physically and spiritually.

Physical comfort - Since the head often gets cold, it can be used daily for comfort and warmth during the last few days of life to keep warm physically.

Spiritual comfort - A prayer shawl or scarf also offers spiritual comfort. It creates a sense of personal space during prayer. It provides reassurance, in a more tangible way, of the presence of the Lord that is with them through the Holy Spirit. By placing it on their head, wrapping it around them, or laying it on them it creates a sense of comfort.

Not Exclusive to Any Religion or Faith

The prayer shawl is not exclusive to any religion or faith. However, the specific design of the Jewish prayer shawl, called the 'tallit,' is used in the Messianic Jewish/Christian faith, strengthening the Believer's ties to the Hebrew roots from where it originated.

The Jewish tallit represents the Word and promises of God. (Numbers 15:37-41) Drawing the shawl over the head of the person who is praying/dying creates a sacred space and is a reminder of God's protection. Women may also enjoy wearing a tallit, or a long scarf like shawl.

Intimacy with God

The prayer shawl is a symbol of intimacy with God. Through the symbolism found throughout the Word, it shows His protection: "covered with His feathers," "under His wings," "lovely tents," "prayer closet."

> *He will cover you with his feathers, and under his wings*
> *you will find refuge; his faithfulness will be*
> *your shield and rampart. Psalm 91:4 NIV*

> *May the LORD repay your work, and may you receive*
> *a rich reward from the LORD, the God of Israel, under*
> *whose wings you have taken refuge." Ruth 2:12 NIV*

For in the day of trouble He will hide me in His shelter;
He will conceal me under the cover of His tent;
He will set me high upon a rock. Psalm 27:5 BSB

In Scripture, the tallit is at times referred to as a 'tent.' The view of all the Israelites praying with their tallits pulled over their heads is described as tents in the Book of Numbers.

How lovely are your tents, O Jacob,
your dwellings, O Israel! Numbers 24:5 BSB

Some believe that Yeshua's command to enter the secret place, our prayer closet, when in prayer referred to being covered with a prayer shawl.

"But you, when you pray, go into your room, and when
you have shut your door, pray to your Father who is
in the secret place; and your Father who sees
in secret will reward you openly." Matthew 6:6 NKJ

Both the tallit and the prayer scarf provide a blessing and privacy to the one wearing it. It helps set the intention and focus of their prayers.

Feeling an Attachment to the Holy Land

If your loved one is familiar with the Hebrew roots of the Christian faith or has been to Israel, they will likely feel an attachment to the Holy Land and to God when they are wearing the tallit or prayer scarf, increasing their sense of God's love and security.

Adorning Your Loved One with the Prayer Shawl

Example:

As you place the prayer shawl or scarf on your loved one's head or body bless them with these types of prayers:

Prayers:

"May God's grace be upon this shawl. Lord God, as we wrap our loved one in a symbol of Your love, we thank You that they are safely under Your wings of protection."

"May this mantle of God's love warm, comfort, enfold, and embrace our loved one at this time."

"Be with our loved one as they recall and relive their life and the issues that need to be addressed before they leave."

"Let this mantle be a safe haven, a sacred place of security and well-being as they go through the labor of dying."

"Cover our loved one with hope, surround them in joy, adorn them with the love and peace of our Lord Jesus Christ, Yeshua ha Mashiach. So be it."

Blessing:

"May God continue to bless you and give you grace, wisdom, and strength along your journey. We pray these things in the Name and authority of Yeshua."

~ 14 ~
Participating in Holy Communion Together

Friends and family can take part in Communion, or the Last Supper, together to remember Yeshua's life, death, and resurrection to eternal life, giving their dying loved one hope and 'food' for their final journey.

Holy Communion is also called "the Lord's Supper," "Cup of Blessing," "Breaking of Bread," and "the Lord's Table." It was called "Eucharist" or giving of thanks in the early Church.

It is also referred to as "the Last Supper" as it was the last meal Yeshua had with His disciples before He left them. We are reminded of this when we celebrate The Last Supper with our loved one.

Food for the Journey

In the Catholic Church the last holy communion before death is called the Viaticum, "food for the journey," keeping in mind that death is a journey into the afterlife.

Catholic Guideline

From the CATHOLIC GUIDELINES FOR THE DYING: Viaticum, Food for the Journey: "When the Eucharist is given to someone who is in danger of death, it is called, 'Viaticum.' The celebration of the Eucharist as viaticum, food for the passage through death to eternal life, is the sacrament proper to the dying Christian. It is the completion and crown of the Christian life on this Earth, signifying that the Christian follows the Lord to eternal glory and the banquet of the heavenly kingdom. The sacrament of the anointing of the sick should be celebrated at the beginning of a serious illness. Viaticum, celebrated when death is close, will then be better understood as the last sacrament of Christian life."

Yeshua Ate His Last Meal

Yeshua ate His last meal at the Feast of Passover before His death. Yeshua instituted the eating of the bread and drinking of the cup at His Last Supper with His disciples. He told us why we celebrate it when He said, "Do this in remembrance of Me," as recalled in First Corinthians:

For I received from the Lord what I also passed on to you: The Lord Jesus, on the night He was betrayed, took bread, and when He had given thanks, He broke it and said, "This is My body, which is for you; do this in remembrance of Me."

*In the same way, after supper He took the cup, saying,
"This cup is the new covenant in My blood; do this, as
often as you drink it, in remembrance of Me." For as
often as you eat this bread and drink this cup, you
proclaim the Lord's death until He comes.*
1 Corinthians 11:23-26 BSB

*While they were eating, Jesus took bread,
spoke a blessing and broke it, and gave it to the disciples,
saying, "Take and eat; this is My body." Then He took
the cup, gave thanks, and gave it to them,
saying, "Drink from it, all of you. This is My blood of
the covenant, which is poured out for many for the
forgiveness of sins. I tell you, I will not drink of this
fruit of the vine from now on until that day when I
drink it anew with you in My Father's kingdom."
And when they had sung a hymn, they went out to the
Mount of Olives. Matthew 26:26-30 BSB*

Partaking of the Last Supper

Giving our loved one an occasion to take part in the Last Supper
is an opportunity for them to present themselves before the Lord
and recognize the eternal life He has given humanity through
His death, burial, and resurrection.

The bread and wine are tangible, visible reminders of Christ's
love. When we take communion, we are remembering Christ's
death on The Tree of Sacrifice and the blood that He shed for
mankind once and for all. This was the fulfillment of the Feast
of Passover in the Hebrew Scriptures. Yeshua gave us a way to
remember this act through this ritual commemorating His Last
Supper with His disciples.

Examining Our Hearts

Before we partake in the elements, it is important for every person to search their own hearts to see if there is unconfessed sin or forgiveness needed. It is a time to purify ourselves on the inside.

This allows time for our loved one to think of any final amends that need to be made and to resolve them with the Lord.

Let a person examine himself, then, and so eat of the bread and drink of the cup. 1 Corinthians 11:28 ESV

People from all walks of life and faiths can cleanse their souls by confessing their sins to God and repenting. Confession is one of the Last Sacraments of the Catholic Church.

And the prayer offered in faith will make the sick person well; the Lord will raise them up. If they have sinned, they will be forgiven. Therefore confess your sins to each other and pray for each other so that you may be healed. The prayer of a righteous person is powerful and effective. James 5:15-16 NIV

Prayer:

"Lord, forgive me for any known and unknown sin that I have committed against You or against others."

~ 15 ~
Officiating the Last Supper

Your prayer and celebration of the Last Supper can be fashioned after the words of the Lord and His apostles when they took part in the bread and cup as written in 1 Corinthians 11:23-26 and Matthew 26:26-29, per the following example.

If your loved one is unresponsive or can no longer eat or drink, they can participate vicariously.

You can place your hand on your loved one's shoulder, or hold their hand, and include them as you and the others partake of the elements.

Taking the Elements

Read the portion of the Scripture, then lead in the partaking of the bread and cup.

Read:

The Lord Jesus, on the night He was betrayed, took bread, and when He had given thanks, He broke it and said, "This is My body, which is for you; do this in remembrance of Me."

Partake – instruct to take the bread:

Say: *"Let us take the bread."*

As each person takes the bread, say:

"Jesus took bread, and when he had given thanks, he broke it and gave it to his disciples, saying, 'Take and eat; this is my body.'"

Say: *"Let us eat the bread with thanksgiving."*

Eat the bread.

Read:

In the same way, after supper He took the cup, saying, "This cup is the new covenant in My blood; do this, as often as you drink it, in remembrance of Me."

Partake – instruct to take the cup:

Say: *"Let us take the cup."*

As each person takes the cup, say:

"Then he took a cup, and when he had given thanks, he gave it to them, saying, 'Drink from it, all of you.'"

Say: *"Let us drink the cup with thanksgiving."*

Drink the cup.

Read:

"For as often as you eat this bread and drink this cup, you proclaim the Lord's death until He comes."

Prayer:

"Thank You, Lord for Your bread and wine, from Heaven, which nourishes us each day of our lives, physically and spiritually, and is nourishing our loved one on their journey to You now."

Participating together in communion gives everyone hope to one day to be together again, seated at the heavenly banquet with all their loved ones.

Additional Scripture

This is the bread that comes down from heaven, so that one may eat of it and not die. I am the living bread that came down from heaven. If anyone eats of this bread, he will live forever. And the bread that I will give for the life of the world is my flesh." John 6:50-51 ESV

I tell you, I will not drink from this fruit of the vine from now on until that day when I drink it new with you in my Father's kingdom. Matthew 26:29 BSB

Let us rejoice and be glad and give Him the glory. For the marriage of the Lamb has come, and His bride has made herself ready. Revelation 19:7 BSB

"Blessed are those who are invited to the marriage supper of the Lamb." Revelation 19:9 BSB

A Sacred Space for Your Loved One

You have now created a sacred space for your loved one. Through preparing everything, purifying, anointing, adorning, and taking part in Holy Communion, you have performed a ceremony that has created a Spirit-filled atmosphere. You can rest assured that your loved one is in a protected, loving environment.

Now you can spend time together in prayer, reading Scripture, singing praise songs, playing music, having a loving family time together, sharing stories of your loved one, or recalling events you experienced together.

And when they had sung a hymn, they went out to the Mount of Olives. Matthew 26:30 BSB

Relive memories of your life together, tell them how much you love them, ask them to forgive you for any hurt you have caused them, forgive them for the times they hurt you.

Sealing Your Time Together

Close your time together with prayer to seal the spiritual work that was done - the purification, anointing, the various acts of faith including the breaking of the bread, the drinking of the cup, and the love that was shared by all.

The special events of this ceremony will be documented in your loved one's Book of Life, at the end of the last chapter of their life on this Earth. It will also be added to your Book of Life, as a special event in the current chapter of your Book, which continues to be written and recorded. This is your Book that will be reviewed one day in your future too.

Prayer:

"Lord, thank you for this special time we have experienced with You and our loved one. We thank You for guiding and directing their journey to You and the afterlife from the heavens above."

"Be with our friends and family and help them to let go of our loved one and find peace in their hearts knowing that their step into eternity will be safe. Help us all to know more of the life that You have for us and what it means during our lifetime on earth.".

"We thank You for the love that was shared and the sacred memory that was created."

The Aaronic Blessing

Conclude your ceremony time by blessing your dying loved one, as well as everyone else in the room with the simple, yet powerful blessing God gave to Moses that was spoken over the people of Israel by his brother Aaron, the first High Priest, thereby called the Aaronic Blessing.

The following is from Numbers 6:24-26 BSB, with the Messianic ending* included.

Bless the people:

"May the LORD bless you and keep you;
may the LORD cause His face to shine upon you
and be gracious to you;
may the LORD lift up His countenance toward you
and give you peace."
*Perfect Peace, in the Name of Yeshua the Messiah,
b'Shem Yeshua ha Mashiach, the Prince of Peace, the
Sar Shalom.

Calling on the Power of God

The symbols and rituals highlighted here are used to make a connection to the spiritual and to bring in the presence of God through the Holy Spirit.

When we cleanse with water, anoint with oil, light candles, cover with the tallit or prayer scarf, and take part in communion we set an atmosphere for the Spirit of God to freely guide our loved one through the transition process. It helps our loved one draw closer to the spiritual part of their lives.

We are also calling upon the power of God and His angels, the Holy Spirit, and Yeshua our Savior for a peaceful release of our loved one's soul and spirit from this earthly realm and their welcomed arrival into Heaven.

~ 16 ~

Additional Items to Incorporate

In addition to the items and rituals discussed previously, you may want to include other things to personalize the atmosphere according to your loved one's personality, preferences, wants, and needs.

Personalize Your Loved One's Experience

- ♥ Other symbols to build faith such as a Cross, a rosary, essential oils or incense for fragrance, crystals like rose quartz for love and forgiveness, flowers, plants, or family pictures can help create a comfortable homelike setting.

- ♥ Handmade passage blankets, which are smaller hand knitted or crocheted blankets, bring extra comfort to hospice patients and are a keepsake to remember your loved one afterwards.

♥ Letters written to your loved one can be read aloud to them while you are sitting vigil.

♥ Soft music playing in the background. You can sing songs.

...be filled with the Spirit, addressing one another in psalms and hymns and spiritual songs, singing and making melody to the Lord with your heart, giving thanks always and for everything to God the Father in the name of our Lord Jesus Christ...
Ephesians 5:18-20 ESV

Read Scripture as Led

Saying prayers and reading Scripture may be done over a period of hours or days as you keep vigil at the bedside of your loved one who is preparing to go home to the Lord. The prayers will console the dying and give comfort to those who tend to them.

"Do not let your hearts be troubled. You believe in God; believe also in me. My Father's house has many rooms; if that were not so, would I have told you that I am going there to prepare a place for you? And if I go and prepare a place for you, I will come back and take you to be with me that you also may be where I am. You know the way to the place where I am going."
John 14:1-4 BSB

Additional Prayers and Scriptures are included in Chapters 22 through 25 to speak or read for direction, comfort, peace, and blessings.

~ 17 ~
Daily Spiritual Care

Once you have established the spiritual atmosphere through performing the rituals you can refresh the spiritual atmosphere each day as led by:

- ♥ Beginning each day with a prayer at the bedside of your loved one – every morning, afternoon, and evening as led.

- ♥ Being present with your loved one at their bedside. Let them know you are there.

- ♥ Daily prayer and Scripture reading.

- ♥ Anointing them with oil.

- ♥ Daily hand holding.

- ♥ Attending to their needs.

- ♥ Reassuring them that everything is happening the way it is supposed to happen.

Pray without ceasing. 1 Thessalonians 5:17 BSB

The Lord's Prayer

Our Father in heaven, Hallowed be Your name.
Your kingdom come. Your will be done
On earth as it is in heaven.
Give us this day our daily bread.
And forgive us our debts, as we forgive our debtors.
And do not lead us into temptation,
But deliver us from the evil one.
For Yours is the kingdom and the power
and the glory forever. Amen.
Matthew 6:9-13 NKJV

The Hail Mary

Hail Mary, full of grace, the Lord is with thee.
Blessed art thou among all women
and blessed is the fruit of thy womb, Jesus.
Holy Mary, Mother of God, pray for us sinners,
now and at the hour of our death.
Amen.

The Apostle's Creed

I believe in God, the Father Almighty, creator of heaven and
earth. I believe in Jesus Christ, His only Son, Our Lord.
He was conceived by the power of the Holy Spirit,
and born of the Virgin Mary.
He suffered under Pontius Pilate, was crucified, died, and was
buried. He descended to the dead.
On the third day He rose again. He ascended into heaven,
and is seated at the right hand of the Father.
He will come again to judge the living and the dead.
I believe in the Holy Spirit, the holy Catholic Church,
the communion of saints, the forgiveness of sins,
the resurrection of the body, and life everlasting.
Amen.

The Serenity Prayer

God, grant me the serenity
to accept the things I cannot change,
the courage to change the things I can,
and the wisdom to know the difference.
Living one day at a time,
enjoying one moment at a time;
accepting hardship as a pathway to peace;
taking, as Jesus did,
this sinful world as it is,
not as I would have it;
trusting that You will make all things right
if I surrender to Your will;
so that I may be reasonably happy in this life
and supremely happy with You forever in the next. Amen.
-Reinhold Niebuhr

Instrument of Your Peace

Lord, make me an instrument of your peace.
Where there is hatred, let me sow love,
Where there is injury, pardon
Where there is doubt, faith,
Where there is despair, hope,
Where there is darkness, light,
Where there is sadness, joy.
O Divine Master, grant that I may not so much
seek to be consoled as to console,
not so much to be understood as to understand,
not so much to be loved, as to love;
for it is in giving that we receive,
it is in pardoning that we are pardoned,
it is in dying that we awake to eternal life.
- Prayer of St. Francis of Assisi

Saying prayers and reading
Scripture may be done over
a period of hours or days as
you keep vigil at the bedside of
your loved one who is preparing
to go home to the Lord.
The prayers will console the dying
and give comfort to those who
tend to them.

~ 18 ~
If Your Loved One's Death is Delaying

If death is prolonged, your loved one may be experiencing spiritual conflict or pain that is keeping them from leaving.

- ♥ They may have some issues from their life review that still need to be resolved.

- ♥ These issues can be words left unsaid, amends that have not been made, or any other unfinished business.

- ♥ They may be in fear over the uncertainty of what is happening.

- ♥ They may not be ready to leave their earthly loved ones.

- ♥ Heaven may not be ready for them just yet.

You can help your loved one through this time even if they are unresponsive. Repeating some of the rituals you have already performed, such as lighting a candle or anointing with oil, can give them peace and help them release. Remember that they can still hear you.

Ask for Help from the Holy Spirit and the Angels

In addition, you can pray and ask God to send His Holy Spirit and the angels to help in the separation process.

- ♥ Ask for your loved one to be able to detach from their family and friends, or anything else that may be still holding them to this world.

- ♥ Ask the Holy Spirit and angels to help any other family members that are having a challenging time letting go to be able to release their loved one.

- ♥ Ask the Holy Spirit to show your loved one the beauty of Heaven and that there is nothing to fear.

- ♥ Ask that they be assured that they are forgiven and loved.

- ♥ Ask for the Love and Light of Heaven to fill everyone so all can sense the spiritual, eternal wonder of the process.

In addition, you can talk to your loved one in a practical way and remind them of what is happening.

Encourage and Reassure Your Loved One

You can encourage and reassure your loved one by gently taking their hand, reminding them of who you are, and giving them guidance and assurance through telling them these types of statements as needed:

- ♥ We love you. We are here to support you.

- ♥ You are dying. This is what it is like to die.

- ♥ We understand that you must go. We will miss you and will always remember you. We will see you again.

- ♥ It is time for you to go now. It is your time to go to Heaven.

- ♥ Everything is happening the way it is supposed to happen. You can relax.

- ♥ You are doing a good job. You can leave all your failures and mistakes behind and take the good with you. You are forgiven.

- ♥ You can leave whenever you are ready. Everyone understands that you must go. We love you so much.

- ♥ Everyone is going to be all right. It is time for you to go to your next home.

- ♥ Look for God's Light, go toward the Light of God. Find His love, peace and understanding in it.

- ♥ You are not alone. There are other loved ones that have gone before that are coming to guide and take you to your new home. Ask for help and they will come!

♥ Do you see any loved ones yet?

Encourage your loved one to visualize a family member that has gone before, to see them running toward them excitedly, greeting them, and welcoming them home saying,

> "We've been waiting for you! So good to see you! Come and see your new home!"

If your loved one has told you that they have seen someone already, remind them of that person coming to greet them. Perhaps an angel will come.

> *"The time came when the beggar died and the angels carried him to Abraham's side." Luke 16:22 NIV*

Help your loved one to visualize themselves seeing Yeshua face to face and feeling His love. No guilt, no shame, no judgement. Pure unconditional love.

Other family and friends that will be visiting or sitting vigil can encourage your loved one again as necessary.

This is an especially crucial time in the life of your loved one. They are doing the labor of dying and you are offering your loving support to help them.

~ 19 ~
At the Actual Death

Commit Your Loved One's Spirit and Soul to God

After your loved one's last breath, or when you have confirmed that your loved one has passed, anoint them with oil on their forehead and all areas of their body as you feel led, to anoint and commit their spirit and soul to God.

> *Then Jesus, calling out with a loud voice, said, "Father, into your hands I commit my spirit!" And having said this he breathed his last. Luke 23:46 ESV*

Example:

As you anoint your loved one with oil, pray this in a similar fashion:

Prayer:

"We commit our loved one's spirit and soul to You, Lord God, the God of Abraham, Isaac, and Jacob through Yeshua ha Mashiach. We ask that our loved one's soul be protected and find peace and joy as it moves to its new home with You. We pray that our loved one is led by Your light. Let them have a wonderful reunion with the loved ones that are already there."

You may touch your loved one, kiss your loved one, or just spend time sitting at the bedside for a few moments. Some people make a toast to their loved one after they pass.

If You Are Not in the Room

When people die, they die at the right time.

If they are private people, they will probably want to leave when no one else is in the room or watching.

Others wait for their loved ones to arrive from out of town, and then after they have seen them, they die.

Still others send people out of the room for something and then depart while they are out fetching the items!

Each death happens the way it is supposed to happen. If you are not in the room when your loved one actually dies, then it was meant to be that way. If you are with your loved one when they pass, cherish the moment. That is the way it was supposed to happen for each of you.

For I know the plans I have for you, declares the LORD, plans to prosper you and not to harm you, to give you a future and a hope. Jeremiah 29:11 BSB

~ 20 ~
Rituals Following Death

There is no need to rush off after the death of your loved one has occurred. You and your family can spend the time needed to say goodbye to them and reflect on what has just happened.

The time right after death can be a time to thank God for your loved one's life. To praise God for His eternal life and His power. To thank Him for watching over your loved one.

It is a time to revel in the warmth of God's love that can be felt permeating the entire room. It is a time to remember all the wonders that have occurred throughout your loved one's dying process. It is a time to recall the evidence of the spiritual presence of God that you experienced.

Say goodbye. Vow to carry on with your life, just as your loved one is starting anew with theirs.

Suggestions for Honoring after Death

There may be traditions and customs you follow for honoring the life of a loved one that has just passed that you may want to implement at this time. In addition, you can:

- ♥ Light a candle and place it near the bed.
- ♥ Toast your loved one's life.
- ♥ Bathe and prepare them.
- ♥ Place a passage blanket on them.
- ♥ Place a flower on the bed after their body has been removed.
- ♥ Take photos of the room to remember the special moments that happened there.

You can also arrange the flowers, the pictures, and other memorable items from the room on the passage blanket and take a photo of everything all together to memorialize this special time. These photos can bring comfort to you later and bring back loving memories as you go through the grieving process.

Praying for the Deceased

In the Jewish faith they sit 'shiva' for seven days after the death of their loved one. It is seven days of mourning and grieving for their dearly departed. However, it is also seven days to continue to support the deceased through their transition. They continue uplifting their loved one in case they are having a challenging time letting go of their earthly life and want to hang on even after they have passed. Those sitting shiva pray for God to help their loved one to detach as appropriate and make a safe journey. They pray for their departed loved one to be able to find peace.

Keeping your loved one in your thoughts and prayers for a period of time believing in a safe journey can be healing both for the deceased and those who remain.

Forgiving Others that Have Passed

The period of reflection after death is a suitable time to ask for or seek forgiveness from someone that the Holy Spirit brings to mind. Perhaps there is a friend, or another loved one that has already passed that you were not on good terms with at the time. Now is an ideal time to take care of this while the windows of Heaven are open for such transactions.

Lighting Candles for Remembrance

The purpose of lighting a candle at the time of death is to pay tribute to the life whose spirit has "passed." It shines light on the darkness of death and symbolizes the light of God in the afterlife.

Throughout the year, lighting a candle and burning it in remembrance of your loved one signifies that their memory still lives on and burns bright in your heart.

A Yahrzeit candle is a candle that burns for 24 hours and is lit each year on the anniversary of your loved one's death in remembrance of their life.

You can also arrange the flowers,

the pictures, and other memorable

items from the room on

the passage blanket and take a photo

of everything all together

to memorialize this special time.

These photos can bring comfort

to you later and bring back

loving memories as you

go through the grieving process.

~ 21 ~
Sudden Death

If your loved one has died suddenly and unexpectedly you can still perform these rituals with the thought of them in mind. You can connect with them through prayer and faith in the Holy Spirit to bring some closure to the sudden death. You can continue to help your loved one separate and make their transition by sending them your love and support from this side of Heaven.

If your loved one has died suddenly without warning, they will be going through the life review on the other side without having the time on Earth to make amends. They most likely will be startled at what happened, but they will have the help of loved ones that have gone before, as well as angels, and Yeshua who will be there to help them through the process.

In the case of sudden death, you can speak with your loved one through the Holy Spirit. The Spirit can share what needs to be said spiritually. It is like mental telepathy in a way – spiritual telepathy!

You can ask and believe that the Spirit will relay your message to your loved one. Believe that they can hear you and you can hear them witnessed by an inner knowing or intuition. You can share what is in your heart with your loved one in thoughts and words through the Spirit especially within the first few days of their death.

In the same way, the Spirit helps us in our weakness.
For we do not know how we ought to pray, but the Spirit
Himself intercedes for us with groans too deep for
words. And He who searches our hearts knows
the mind of the Spirit, because the Spirit intercedes
for the saints according to the will of God.
Romans 8:26-27 ESV

Release Your Loved One

It is important to release your loved one. Let them go so their spirit and soul will not linger. Forgive them for anything that was unresolved in your relationship. Be hopeful that you will see them again one day when you arrive in eternity.

Continue to pray for them in the days and weeks ahead as they continue their life review. Ask for them to be released from this world and find the love and the new life in Heaven. Let them know everyone will be all right. Let them know you love them and what they mean to you.

The possibility of sudden death is why it is important to keep any negative accounts we have with others short. It is important to forgive and ask for forgiveness and to love one another whenever, however possible.

It is best to forgive while we are still alive, but many times we will not be able to. Thankfully even after death, we can still ask for forgiveness as well as forgive through the Spirit.

You may or may not feel instantaneous peace, but you can believe that you have communicated with each other in the Spirit. You can continue to speak to each other throughout your lifetime as needed. In the meantime, be comforted in knowing that your love has been expressed and that any needed amends will be made between you. Your hearts have spoken, life will continue, and all will be well.

"Have compassion

for our loved one and calm

their anxious cries and groans.

Give them peace.

Let them see Your kingdom

and the place that

You have graciously prepared

for them from the beginning

of this age."

PART FOUR

~ 22 ~
Prayers

Pray the following prayers to God, our Creator, as led by the Spirit, inserting your loved one's name into the prayer.

Prayer to Know Yeshua Before Dying

"Heavenly Father, we pray for the salvation of our loved one who is close to death. If they do not know You personally, we ask that as they face the end of their life on this Earth, You make Yourself known to them."

"May they confess their sins and receive forgiveness. May they believe in their heart and confess with their mouth that Your shed blood, death, and resurrection have made a way for them to live forever with You."

"Lord Jesus, Come into our loved one's life. Cleanse them from all unrighteousness. Move into their heart. Let them receive You as their Lord and Savior. So be it."

Believing that hearing is the last sense to go, you can ask your loved one to accept the Lord as their Savior in their heart, even if they cannot respond outwardly. God will hear them.

Short Prayers and Intentions for Your Loved One

"Heavenly Father, let our loved one know Your love as they make their journey to Heaven. Surround them with Your love."

"Help our loved one to know that You are with them during this time of transition. Give peace to their soul and spirit as they move into the afterlife. "

"Make our loved one's passage easy. Give them the strength and grace they need to face the issues of life their heart needs to put to rest."

Keep thy heart with all diligence;
For out of it are the issues of life. Proverbs 4:23 ASV

"Send the Spirit of Truth to bring clarity to the issues of life that need to be addressed and understood."

"Deliver our loved one from all anguish and distress, release them from this Earth and take them to Yourself in Your Kingdom."

"Have compassion for our loved one and calm their anxious cries and groans. Give them peace. Let them see Your kingdom and the place that You have graciously prepared for them from the beginning of this age."

"Help them to make peace with themselves and others during this time."

"Give them the ability to forgive any people that have hurt them, physically or emotionally."

"Blot out their transgressions from the Book of Remembrance."

"Bless our loved one for the love they have given to others throughout their life."

"Let love be expressed with their friends and family. Let their final times of sharing love with each other be blessed."

"Help our loved one to detach from the hold that life may have on them."

"Send angels to help them to let go of this world and move to the next with nothing unsaid or undone. Let the last chapter of their Book of Life on Earth be recorded as 'finished well.'"

"Let them see the truth in all matters of their life and understand the purposes for which they happened."

"Let the goodbyes be filled with love and hope for a future together again one day."

"We ask for the loved ones who are already there in Heaven to be with our loved one to help them with their transition."

"Thank You Lord that You have been preparing a place for our loved one."

"We ask for a warm welcome to the next phase of their eternal life."

"We ask these things through Yeshua ha Mashiach, Jesus the Christ, Your Holy Son, our Lord, Savior, and Redeemer. So be it."

Prayers for Knowing How to Help Our Loved One

"Help us to create a sacred environment for our loved one while they are passing."

"Let us be sensitive to our loved one's physical and spiritual needs. Help us to know when to stop giving food, water, and meds. Help us to know when to pray with them and comfort them."

"Help us to make the most of every moment together and realize that simply holding our loved one's hand is one of the most important things we can do."

"Help us to be able to calm any fears our loved one may have."

"Help us to guide them to the truth through Your Word."

"Creator God, be a witness of the eternal life that awaits those who call on Your Name."

A Prayer for the Family of the Deceased

"Father God, be with our loved one and our family at this time. Provide us with Your comfort. We pray for peace knowing that our loved one is in Your care. We are thankful that our loved one is at rest. We are thankful for eternal life."

"Lord God, let us feel Your presence. Send the Comforter to console us in our time of mourning. Help us to understand what has happened and what life is truly about. Heal our hearts from the loss of our loved one."

"Let us continue to know Your love. Thank You for caring for each and every one of us. We believe You will give us strength and direction as we carry on this life You have given us. We love you, Lord."

"Thank You for the gift that our loved one is to us in our lives. They will always live in our hearts. Thank You for the promise that we will be with our loved one again."

"We love you _____ (loved one). Until we meet again, peace be with you and our/your family."

"Thank You for the gift that
our loved one is to us in our lives.
They will always live in our hearts.
Thank You for the promise
that we will be with
our loved one again."

~ 23 ~
Scriptures for Assurance and Comfort

Bible Verses to Build Faith During Hospice

Reading passages of the Bible to someone that is at the end of their life can be immensely helpful, lifting up the situation for everyone involved. Scripture has a spiritual power that can make your loved one feel safe, give them hope, and bring comfort.

Keeping a Vigil

Scripture can also be read aloud or silently while keeping a vigil for your loved one. A vigil is where you stay with your loved one, in the room or alongside the bedside, and quietly wait, and pray, and keep watch over them for an extended period of time. A night vigil sometimes includes a candle and is thereby called a candlelight vigil.

The following verses and passages of Scripture can bring answers, comfort, and healing to the person who is dying, as well as to the family and those at their bedside. Read through them over time or look for selected verses that are right for the current moment to give peace, direction, and assurance.

Short Verses

Who shall separate us from the love of Christ?
Romans 8:35 NIV

Our help is in the name of the LORD,
the Maker of heaven and earth. Psalm 124:8 NIV

If we live, we live for the Lord;
and if we die, we die for the Lord.
So, whether we live or die, we belong to the Lord.
Romans 14:8 NIV

In you, LORD my God, I put my trust. Psalm 25:1 NIV

Search me, O God, and know my heart; test me and know
my concerns. See if there is any offensive way in me;
lead me in the way everlasting. Psalm 139:23-24 BSB

Be kind and compassionate to one another,
forgiving each other, just as in Christ God forgave you.
Ephesians 4:31-32 NIV

I can do all things through Christ who gives me strength.
Philippians 4:13 ESV

And so we will be with the Lord forever.
1 Thessalonians 4:17 NIV

Even though I walk through the darkest valley,
I will fear no evil, for you are with me. Psalm 23:4 NIV

Jesus, remember me when you come into your kingdom.
Luke 23:42 NIV

Into your hands I commit my spirit. Psalm 31:6 NIV

Lord Jesus, receive my spirit. Acts 7:59 ESV

And now these three remain: faith, hope and love.
But the greatest of these is love. 1 Corinthians 13:13 NIV

You will make known to me the way of life;
In Your presence is fullness of joy; In Your right hand
there are pleasures forever. Psalm 16:11 NAS

Jesus said to him, "I am the way, and the truth, and the life.
No one comes to the Father except through me."
John 14:6 ESV

"My Father's house has many rooms; if that were not so,
would I have told you that I am going there
to prepare a place for you?" John 14:2 NIV

God is our refuge and strength,
an ever-present help in times of trouble. Psalm 46:1 NIV

What then shall we say in response to these things?
If God is for us, who can be against us? Romans 8:31 NIV

The grace of the Lord Jesus Christ, and the love of God,
and the communion of the Holy Spirit, be with you all.
2 Corinthians 13:14 ASV

"Father God, be with our loved one

and our family at this time.

Provide us with Your comfort.

We pray for peace in knowing that

our loved one is in Your care.

We are thankful that

our loved one is at rest.

We are thankful for eternal life."

~ 24 ~
Faith, Hope, Love, and Forgiveness

First Corinthians Thirteen (NIV)

*If I speak in the tongues of men or of angels,
but do not have love, I am only
a resounding gong or a clanging cymbal.*

*If I have the gift of prophecy
and can fathom all mysteries and all knowledge,
and if I have a faith that can move mountains,
but do not have love, I am nothing.*

*If I give all I possess to the poor and give over
my body to hardship that I may boast,
but do not have love, I gain nothing.*

*Love is patient, love is kind.
It does not envy, it does not boast, it is not proud.
It does not dishonor others, it is not self-seeking, it is not
easily angered, it keeps no record of wrongs.*

Love does not delight in evil but rejoices with the truth.
It always protects, always trusts, always hopes,
always perseveres.

Love never fails. But where there are prophecies,
they will cease; where there are tongues, they will be stilled;
where there is knowledge, it will pass away.

For we know in part and we prophesy in part, but when
completeness comes, what is in part disappears.

When I was a child, I talked like a child, I thought like a child,
I reasoned like a child. When I became a man,
I put the ways of childhood behind me.

For now we see only a reflection as in a mirror;
then we shall see face to face.
Now I know in part; then I shall know fully,
even as I am fully known.

And now these three remain: faith, hope and love. But the
greatest of these is love.

Faith - The Substance of Things Hoped for

Now faith is the substance of things hoped for,
the evidence of things not seen. Hebrews 11:1 NKJ

It is God who justifies. Who then is the one who condemns?
No one. Christ Jesus who died—more than that,
who was raised to life—is at the right hand of God
and is also interceding for us. Romans 8:33-34 NIV

"For I have come down from heaven, not to do My own will,
but to do the will of Him who sent Me. And this is the will of
Him who sent Me, that I shall lose none of those He has given
Me, but raise them up at the last day. For it is My Father's
will that everyone who looks to the Son and believes in Him
shall have eternal life, and I will raise him up at the last day."
John 6:38-40 BSB

Jesus said to her, "I am the resurrection and the life.
The one who believes in me will live, even though they die;
and whoever lives by believing in me will never die.
Do you believe this?" John 11:25-26 NIV

"Father, I want those you have given me to be with me where
I am, and to see my glory, the glory you have given me
because you loved me before the creation of the world."
John 17:24 NIV

"He will wipe every tear from their eyes. There will be no
more death' or mourning or crying or pain, for the old order
of things has passed away." Revelation 21:4 NIV

"I know that my redeemer lives, and that in the end he will
stand on the earth. And after my skin has been destroyed,
yet in my flesh I will see God; I myself will
see him with my own eyes—I, and not another.
How my heart yearns within me!" Job 19:25-27 BSB

*But our citizenship is in heaven. And we eagerly await a
Savior from there, the Lord Jesus Christ, who, by the power
that enables him to bring everything under his control,
will transform our lowly bodies so that they will be
like his glorious body. Philippians 3:20-21 NIV*

*And we know that God works all things together
for the good of those who love Him, who are called according
to His purpose. For those God foreknew, He also predestined
to be conformed to the image of His Son,
so that He would be the firstborn among many brothers.
And those He predestined, He also called; those He called,
He also justified; those He justified, He also glorified.
Romans 8:28-30 NIV*

*What then shall we say in response to these things?
If God is for us, who can be against us? He who did not spare
His own Son but gave Him up for us all, how will He not also,
along with Him, freely give us all things? Who will bring any
charge against God's elect? It is God who justifies. Who is
there to condemn us? For Christ Jesus, who died, and more
than that was raised to life, is at the right hand of God—
and He is interceding for us. Romans 8:31-34 NIV*

Hope - For Things Yet Unseen

May the God of hope fill you with all joy and peace
as you trust in him, so that you may overflow with hope
by the power of the Holy Spirit. Romans 15:13 NIV

"Where, O death, is your victory?
Where, O death, is your sting?" 1 Corinthians 15:55 NIV

The sting of death is sin, and the power of sin is the law.
But thanks be to God! He gives us the victory through our
Lord Jesus Christ. Therefore, my dear brothers and sisters,
stand firm. Let nothing move you. Always give yourselves fully
to the work of the Lord, because you know that your labor
in the Lord is not in vain. 1 Corinthians 15:56-58 NIV

Yet this I call to mind and therefore I have hope:
Because of the LORD's great love we are not consumed,
for his compassions never fail. They are new every morning;
great is your faithfulness. I say to myself,
"The LORD is my portion; therefore I will wait for him."
Lamentations 3:21-24 NIV

The LORD is good to those whose hope is in him, to the one
who seeks him; it is good to wait quietly for
the salvation of the LORD. Lamentations 3:25-26 NIV

And if the Spirit of him who raised Jesus from the dead is
living in you, he who raised Christ from the dead
will also give life to your mortal bodies
because of his Spirit who lives in you. Romans 8:11 NIV

He has rescued us from the dominion of darkness
and brought us into the kingdom of His beloved Son,
in whom we have redemption, the forgiveness of sins.
Colossians 1:13-14 BSB

113

Love ~ The Greatest of These

The Greatest Commandment

Now one of the scribes had come up and heard their debate.
Noticing how well Jesus had answered them, he asked Him,
"Which commandment is the most important of all?"
Jesus replied, "This is the most important:
'Hear O Israel, the Lord our God, the Lord is One.
Love the Lord your God with all your heart and with all your
soul and with all your mind and with all your strength.'
The second is this: 'Love your neighbor as yourself.' No other
commandment is greater than these." Mark 12:28-31 NIV

"As the Father has loved me, so have I loved you. Now remain
in my love. If you keep my commands, you will remain in my
love, just as I have kept my Father's commands and remain in
his love. I have told you this so that my joy may be in you
and that your joy may be complete." John 15:9-11 NIV

"My command is this:
Love each other as I have loved you.
Greater love has no one than this: to lay down one's life for
one's friends. You are my friends if you do what I command.
I no longer call you servants, because a servant
does not know his master's business.
Instead, I have called you friends,
for everything that I learned from my Father
I have made known to you." John 15:12-15 NIV

"You did not choose me, but I chose you and appointed you
so that you might go and bear fruit—fruit that will last—
and so that whatever you ask in my name
the Father will give you.
This is my command: 'Love each other.'"
John 15:16-17 NIV

Who shall separate us from the love of Christ?
Shall trouble or hardship or persecution or famine
or nakedness or danger or sword? Romans 8:35 NIV

No, in all these things we are more than conquerors
through him who loved us. For I am convinced that neither
death nor life, neither angels nor demons, neither the present
nor the future, nor any powers, neither height nor depth,
nor anything else in all creation, will be able to separate us
from the love of God that is in Christ Jesus our Lord.
Romans 8:37-39 NIV

My goal is that they may be encouraged in heart
and united in love, so that they may have the full riches
of complete understanding, in order that they may know
the mystery of God, namely, Christ, in whom are hidden all
the treasures of wisdom and knowledge. Colossians 2:2-3 NIV

Therefore, as the elect of God, holy and beloved,
clothe yourselves with hearts of compassion, kindness,
humility, gentleness, and patience. Colossians 3:12 BSB

And over all these virtues put on love,
which is the bond of perfect unity. Colossians 3:14 BSB

Be kind to one another, tenderhearted, forgiving one another,
as God in Christ forgave you. Ephesians 4:32 ESV

Forgiveness

Then Jesus said, "Father, forgive them,
for they do not know what they are doing." Luke 23:34 NIV

For you, O Lord, are good and forgiving, abounding
in steadfast love to all who call upon you. Psalm 86:5 ESV

If we confess our sins, he is faithful and just to forgive us
our sins and to cleanse us from all unrighteousness.
1 John 1:9 ESV

He has delivered us from the domain of darkness and
transferred us to the kingdom of his beloved Son,
in whom we have redemption, the forgiveness of sins.
Colossians 1:13-14 ESV

...as far as the east is from the west, so far does he remove
our transgressions from us. Psalm 103:12 ESV

"For if you forgive men their trespasses, your heavenly Father
will also forgive you. But if you do not forgive men their
trespasses, neither will your Father forgive yours."
Matthew 6:14-15 ESV

"I, yes I, am He who blots out your transgressions for My own
sake and remembers your sins no more." Isaiah 43:25 BSB

Bear with one another and forgive any complaint you may
have against someone else. Forgive as the Lord forgave you.
Colossians 3:13 NIV

Blessed is he whose transgressions are forgiven, whose sins
are covered. Blessed is the man whose iniquity the LORD
does not count against him, in whose spirit there is no deceit.
Psalm 32:1-2 BSB

Get rid of all bitterness, rage and anger,
outcry and slander, along with every form of malice.
Be kind and tenderhearted to one another,
forgiving each other just as in Christ God forgave you.
Ephesians 4:31-32 NIV

"Judge not, and you will not be judged;
condemn not, and you will not be condemned:
forgive, and you will be forgiven;
give, and it will be given to you.
Good measure, pressed down, shaken together,
running over, will be put into your lap.
For with the measure you use
it will be measured back to you." Luke 6:37-38 ESV

Then Peter came to Jesus and asked, "Lord, how many times
shall I forgive my brother who sins against me? Up to seven
times?" Jesus answered, "I tell you, not just seven times, but
seventy-seven times!" Matthew 18:21-22 BSB

Eternal Life

That which was from the beginning, which we have heard,
which we have seen with our own eyes,
which we have gazed upon and touched with our own hands—
this is the Word of life. And this is the life that was revealed;
we have seen it and testified to it, and we proclaim to you the
eternal life that was with the Father and was revealed to us.
1 John 1:1-2 BSB

"For God so loved the world that He gave His one and
only Son, that everyone who believes in Him
shall not perish but have eternal life.
For God did not send His Son into the world to condemn
the world, but to save the world through Him.
Whoever believes in Him is not condemned,
but whoever does not believe has already been condemned,
because he has not believed in the name of
God's one and only Son." John 3:16-18 BSB

Truly, truly, I say to you, whoever hears my word and believes
him who sent me has eternal life. He does not come into
judgment, but has passed from death to life. John 5:24 ESV

"Do not work for food that spoils, but for food that endures to
eternal life, which the Son of Man will give you. For on him
God the Father has placed his seal of approval."
John 6:23 NIV

"And I give them eternal life, and they shall never perish;
neither shall anyone snatch them out of My hand."
John 10:28 NKJV

And this is the promise that He Himself made to us:
eternal life.1 John 2:25 BSB

Overcoming Fear

The LORD is my light and my salvation—whom shall I fear?
The LORD is the stronghold of my life—whom shall I dread?
Psalm 27: 1-2 NIV

Be anxious for nothing, but in everything, by prayer and
petition, with thanksgiving, present your requests to God.
And the peace of God, which surpasses all understanding,
will guard your hearts and your minds in Christ Jesus.
Philippians 4:6-7 NIV BSB

Do not fear, for I am with you; do not be afraid, for I am your
God. I will strengthen you; I will surely help you; I will uphold
you with My right hand of righteousness. Isaiah 41:10 NIV

"My sheep listen to My voice; I know them, and they follow
Me. I give them eternal life, and they will never perish.
No one can snatch them out of My hand. My Father who has
given them to Me is greater than all. No one can snatch them
out of My Father's hand. I and the Father are one."
John 10:27-30 NIV

"And I will ask the Father, and He will give you another
Advocate to be with you forever— the Spirit of truth.
The world cannot receive Him, because it neither sees Him
nor knows Him. But you do know Him, for He abides with you
and will be in you. But the Advocate, the Holy Spirit,
whom the Father will send in My name, will teach you all
things and will remind you of everything I have told you."
John 14:16-17, 26 NIV

For to me, to live is Christ, and to die is gain.
But if I go on living in the body, this will mean
fruitful labor for me. So what shall I choose?
I do not know. I am torn between the two.
I desire to depart and be with Christ,
which is far better indeed. Philippians 1:21-23 BSB

Let the peace of Christ rule in your hearts
for to this you were called as members of one body.
And be thankful. Colossians 3:15 NIV

"Be strong and courageous; do not be afraid or terrified
of them, for it is the LORD your God who goes with you;
He will never leave you nor forsake you."
Deuteronomy 31:6 NIV

Now this is what the LORD says—He who created you,
O Jacob, and He who formed you, O Israel:
"Do not fear, for I have redeemed you;
I have called you by your name; you are Mine!"
Isaiah 43:1 NIV

"When you pass through the waters, I will be with you;
and when you go through the rivers, they will not overwhelm
you. When you walk through the fire, you will not be scorched;
the flames will not set you ablaze.
For I am the LORD your God, the Holy One of Israel,
your Savior. Isaiah 43:2-3 NIV

Strength

He gives power to the faint and increases the strength
of the weak. Even youths grow tired and weary,
and young men stumble and fall.
But those who wait upon the LORD will renew their strength;
they will mount up with wings like eagles;
they will run and not grow weary,
they will walk and not faint. Isaiah 40:28-31 ESV

"Have I not commanded you to be strong and courageous?
Do not be afraid; do not be discouraged, for the LORD
your God is with you wherever you go. Joshua 1:9 NIV

Cast your burden upon the LORD and He will sustain you;
He will never let the righteous be shaken. Psalm 55:22 BSB

...being strengthened with all power, according to his glorious
might, for all endurance and patience with joy;
giving thanks to the Father, who has qualified you to share in
the inheritance of the saints in light. Colossians 1:11-12 ESV

But He said to me, "My grace is sufficient for you,
for My power is perfected in weakness."
Therefore I will boast all the more gladly in my weaknesses,
so that the power of Christ may rest on me.
2 Corinthians 12:9 ESV

Trust in the LORD with all your heart and lean not on your
own understanding; in all your ways acknowledge Him,
and He will make your paths straight. Proverbs 3:5-6 ESV

Surely God is my salvation; I will trust and not be afraid.
For the LORD GOD is my strength and my song,
and He also has become my salvation." Isaiah 12:2 ESV

Comfort for the Grieving

"Blessed are those who mourn, for they will be comforted."
Matthew 5:4 ESV

"So also you have sorrow now, but I will see you again,
and your hearts will rejoice, and no one will take
your joy from you." John 16:22 ESV

The LORD is near to the brokenhearted
and saves the crushed in spirit. Psalm 34:18 ESV

"Come to Me, all you who are weary and burdened,
and I will give you rest.
Take My yoke upon you and learn from Me;
for I am gentle and humble in heart,
and you will find rest for your souls. For My yoke is easy
and My burden is light." Matthew 11: 28-30 ESV

... but whoever drinks the water I give them will never thirst.
Indeed, the water I give them will become in them a spring
of water welling up to eternal life." ... John 4:14 NIV

Blessed be the God and Father of our Lord Jesus Christ,
the Father of compassion and the God of all comfort,
who comforts us in all our troubles,
so that we can comfort those in any trouble
with the comfort we ourselves have received from God.
For just as the sufferings of Christ overflow to us, so also
through Christ our comfort overflows.
2 Corinthians 1:3-5 BSB

It is Well with My Soul - Lyrics

Author: Horatio Gates Spafford

When peace like a river, attendeth my way,
When sorrows like sea billows roll;
Whatever my lot, Thou hast taught me to know
It is well, it is well, with my soul.

Refrain
It is well, (it is well),
With my soul, (with my soul)
It is well, it is well, with my soul.

Though Satan should buffet, though trials should come,
Let this blest assurance control,
That Christ has regarded my helpless estate,
And hath shed His own blood for my soul.

My sin, oh, the bliss of this glorious thought!
My sin, not in part but the whole,
Is nailed to the cross, and I bear it no more,
Praise the Lord, praise the Lord, O my soul!

For me, be it Christ, be it Christ hence to live:
If Jordan above me shall roll,
No pang shall be mine, for in death as in life,
Thou wilt whisper Thy peace to my soul.

But Lord, 'tis for Thee, for Thy coming we wait,
The sky, not the grave, is our goal;
Oh, trump of the angel! Oh, voice of the Lord!
Blessed hope, blessed rest of my soul.

And Lord, haste the day when the faith shall be sight,
The clouds be rolled back as a scroll;
The trump shall resound, and the Lord shall descend,
A song in the night, oh my soul!

While you will not be able

to help heal the physical sickness

of your loved one,

you can help them as they

prepare their soul and spirit

to make their ultimate

transition to Eternity.

~ 25 ~
Scripture Passages

The Lord is My Shepherd
Psalm 23 ESV

The LORD is my shepherd; I shall not want.
He makes me lie down in green pastures.

He leads me beside still waters. He restores my soul.
He leads me in paths of righteousness for his name's sake.

Even though I walk through the valley of the shadow of death,
I will fear no evil, for you are with me;
your rod and your staff, they comfort me.

You prepare a table before me in the presence of my enemies;
you anoint my head with oil; my cup overflows.

Surely goodness and mercy
shall follow me all the days of my life,
and I shall dwell in the house of the LORD forever.

Love Comes from God
1 John 4:7-19 NIV

Beloved, let us love one another, because love comes from God. Everyone who loves has been born of God and knows God. Whoever does not love does not know God, because God is love.

This is how God's love was revealed among us: God sent His one and only Son into the world, so that we might live through Him. And love consists in this: not that we loved God, but that He loved us and sent His Son as the atoning sacrifice for our sins.

Beloved, if God so loved us, we also ought to love one another. No one has ever seen God; but if we love one another, God remains in us, and His love is perfected in us.

By this we know that we remain in Him, and He in us: He has given us of His Spirit. And we have seen and testify that the Father has sent His Son to be the Savior of the world.

If anyone confesses that Jesus is the Son of God, God abides in him, and he in God. And we have come to know and believe the love that God has for us.

God is love; whoever abides in love abides in God, and God in him. In this way, love has been perfected among us, so that we may have confidence on the day of judgment; for in this world we are just like Him.

There is no fear in love, but perfect love drives out fear, because fear involves punishment. The one who fears has not been perfected in love. We love because He first loved us.

Help Comes from the Lord
Psalm 121 NIV

I lift up my eyes to the mountains—
where does my help come from?
My help comes from the LORD, the Maker of heaven and earth.
He will not let your foot slip—he who watches over you will
not slumber; indeed, he who watches over Israel
will neither slumber nor sleep.

The LORD watches over you—
the LORD is your shade at your right hand; the sun will not
harm you by day, nor the moon by night.

The LORD will keep you from all harm—
he will watch over your life;
the LORD will watch over your coming and going
both now and forevermore.

Spiritual Wisdom
Ephesians 1:18-23 BSB

I ask that the eyes of your heart may be enlightened,
so that you may know the hope of His calling,
the riches of His glorious inheritance in the saints,
and the surpassing greatness of His power to us who believe.

These are in accordance with the working of His mighty
strength, which He exerted in Christ when He raised Him
from the dead and seated Him at His right hand in the
heavenly realms, far above all rule and authority, power and
dominion, and every name that is named, not only in the
present age but also in the one to come.

And God put everything under His feet and made Him head
over everything for the church, which is His body,
the fullness of Him who fills all in all.

You Have Searched Me and Known Me
Psalm 139:1-12 BSB

O LORD, You have searched me and known me.
You know when I sit and when I rise;
You understand my thoughts from afar.

You search out my path and my lying down;
You are aware of all my ways.
Even before a word is on my tongue,
You know all about it, O LORD.

You hem me in behind and before;
You have laid Your hand upon me.
Such knowledge is too wonderful for me,
too lofty for me to attain.

Where can I go to escape Your Spirit?
Where can I flee from Your presence?

If I ascend to the heavens, You are there;
if I make my bed in Sheol, You are there.
If I rise on the wings of the dawn,
if I settle by the farthest sea,
even there Your hand will guide me;
Your right hand will hold me fast.

If I say, "Surely the darkness will hide me,
and the light become night around me"—
even the darkness is not dark to You,
but the night shines like the day,
for darkness is as light to You.

You Are My Refuge and My Fortress
Psalm 91 BSB

He who dwells in the shelter of the Most High will abide in the shadow of the Almighty. I will say to the LORD, "You are my refuge and my fortress, my God, in whom I trust."

Surely He will deliver you from the snare of the fowler, and from the deadly plague. He will cover you with His feathers; under His wings you will find refuge; His faithfulness is a shield and rampart.

You will not fear the terror of the night, nor the arrow that flies by day, nor the pestilence that stalks in the darkness, nor the calamity that destroys at noon.

Though a thousand may fall at your side, and ten thousand at your right hand, no harm will come near you.

You will only see it with your eyes and witness the punishment of the wicked. Because you have made the LORD your dwelling—my refuge, the Most High—no evil will befall you, no plague will approach your tent.

For He will command His angels concerning you to guard you in all your ways. They will lift you up in their hands, so that you will not strike your foot against a stone.

You will tread on the lion and cobra; you will trample the young lion and serpent.

"Because he loves Me, I will deliver him; because he knows My name, I will protect him. When he calls out to Me, I will answer him; I will be with him in trouble. I will deliver him and honor him. With long life I will satisfy him and show him My salvation."

Where, O Death, Is Your Victory?
1 Corinthians 15:50-54 NIV

*I declare to you, brothers and sisters,
that flesh and blood cannot inherit the kingdom of God,
nor does the perishable inherit the imperishable.*

*Listen, I tell you a mystery:
We will not all sleep, but we will all be changed— in a flash,
in the twinkling of an eye, at the last trumpet.*

*For the trumpet will sound, the dead will be raised
imperishable, and we will be changed.
For the perishable must clothe itself with the imperishable,
and the mortal with immortality.*

*When the perishable has been clothed with the imperishable,
and the mortal with immortality,
then the saying that is written will come true:
"Death has been swallowed up in victory."*

The Year of the Lord's Favor
Isaiah 61:1-3 ESV

*The Spirit of the Lord GOD is on Me, because the LORD has
anointed Me to preach good news to the poor.
He has sent Me to bind up the brokenhearted,
to proclaim liberty to the captives
and freedom to the prisoners,
to proclaim the year of the LORD's favor and the day of our
God's vengeance, to comfort all who mourn,
to console the mourners in Zion—
to give them a crown of beauty for ashes,
the oil of joy for mourning, and a garment of praise
for a spirit of despair.
So they will be called oaks of righteousness,
the planting of the LORD, that He may be glorified.*

The Return of the Lord
1 Thessalonians 4:13-18 ESV

*Brothers, we do not want you to be uninformed about those
who sleep in death, so that you will not grieve like the rest,
who are without hope.*

*For since we believe that Jesus died and rose again,
we also believe that God will bring with Jesus those who have
fallen asleep in Him.*

*By the word of the Lord, we declare to you that we who are
alive and remain until the coming of the Lord will by no
means precede those who have fallen asleep.*

*For the Lord Himself will descend from heaven
with a loud command, with the voice of an archangel,
and with the trumpet of God, and the dead in Christ
will be the first to rise.*

*After that, we who are alive and remain will be caught up
together with them in the clouds to meet the Lord in the air.
And so we will always be with the Lord.
Therefore encourage one another with these words.*

Bless the LORD, O My Soul
Psalm 103 ESV

*Bless the LORD, O my soul, and all that is within me,
bless his holy name!
Bless the LORD, O my soul, and forget not all his benefits,
who forgives all your iniquity, who heals all your diseases,
who redeems your life from the pit,
who crowns you with steadfast love and mercy,
who satisfies you with good
so that your youth is renewed like the eagle's.*

The LORD works righteousness and justice for all
who are oppressed. He made known his ways to Moses,
his acts to the people of Israel. The LORD is merciful and
gracious, slow to anger and abounding in steadfast love.

He will not always chide, nor will he keep his anger forever.
He does not deal with us according to our sins,
nor repay us according to our iniquities.

For as high as the heavens are above the earth,
so great is his steadfast love toward those who fear him;
as far as the east is from the west,
so far does he remove our transgressions from us.

As a father shows compassion to his children,
so the LORD shows compassion to those who fear him.
For he knows our frame; he remembers that we are dust.
As for man, his days are like grass; he flourishes like a flower
of the field; for the wind passes over it,
and it is gone, and its place knows it no more.

But the steadfast love of the LORD
is from everlasting to everlasting on those who fear him,
and his righteousness to children's children, to those who
keep his covenant and remember to do his commandments.

The LORD has established his throne in the heavens,
and his kingdom rules over all.

Bless the LORD, O you his angels, you mighty ones
who do his word, obeying the voice of his word!

Bless the LORD, all his hosts, his ministers, who do his will!

Bless the LORD, all his works,
in all places of his dominion. Bless the LORD, O my soul!

~ 26 ~
Notations - Practical & Spiritual

There are some handy, practical items that can be helpful to have with you when you sit vigil with your loved one.

Journal and a Pen

Having a journal and pen on hand will encourage you to take notes of what and when things happen. You will be going through many new experiences, and they will blur together. These notes will help you recall the special memories that will be forgotten over time.

Make notes of the practical as well as the spiritual revelations you have throughout the time you are supporting your loved one through the labor of dying:

Practical Notes

You can make practical notes to keep track of what needs to be done:

- ♥ Ask your loved one's hospice nurses about the typical physical stages of dying so that you know what to look for, as well as gestures your loved one may make that can be associated with their life review.

- ♥ Note which stage of the dying process your loved one is experiencing.

- ♥ Make notes of what the doctors tell you and what you want to ask them the next time you see them. They come in and go out quickly, so you need to be ready!

- ♥ Start making notes about things as they come to mind that need to be taken care of before and after death occurs, such as people to invite to the memorial service, practical tasks like closing of accounts and moving of personal items.

- ♥ Write down any interesting things your loved one says or does.

- ♥ Determine if your loved one is still responsive to your presence and note when they are no longer.

- ♥ Note any dying words or movements.

Spiritual Revelations

Make notes of the spiritual revelations you receive as your loved one transitions to heaven.

- ♥ What are you discovering through the process of dying?

- ♥ Can you sense the spiritual atmosphere changing?

- ♥ Can you sense your loved one going through the process of leaving their earthly life behind and moving toward their spiritual life?

- ♥ What revelations of the heavenly realm can you sense?

- ♥ Are there Scriptures that come to mind as you go through the dying process with your loved one?

- ♥ Have they mentioned loved ones that have passed before?

- ♥ Can you feel the love among those in the room?

- ♥ If you were in the room, did you feel your loved one's spirit leave their body?

The dying process can be a wonderous experience, and much can be discovered and realized through it.

Many of these notes can be made later when you have time to reflect on it. Write down as much as you can remember as soon as you can though, so you remember the most. Then you can put the notes aside until the time comes when you want to think about the whole experience again and then you will have the memories you need.

Tote Bag

In addition to carrying the items you will be bringing to use for the End-of-Life Ceremony and the other spiritual care activities, there are other unplanned items you will be taking back and forth from the hospital, and a tote bag comes in handy!

Bringing an extra change of clothes and some essential personal toiletries can give you comfort, refreshment, and flexibility when staying overnight.

Visit www.End-of-Life-Spiritual-Care.com for updates.

~ 27 ~
Final Thoughts

Having someone by their side throughout the process of dying is the greatest gift anyone can have.

If you are that 'someone' you have been a tremendous blessing to your loved one. You have helped them during the most important event of their life. You will also have been changed forever by the loving spiritual moments you experienced.

May God Almighty bless you richly for the love you have shown to your loved one – who is one of His children! May He continue to show you more of His wonders each day to build on what you have already discovered through this experience.

~~~~~~~~~~~~~~~~~

If you have a testimony of your loved one's death experience that you would like to share, we would like to hear it! Please email it to: SpiritualCareCollection@gmail.com. We may share it on our book's website!

All Scripture

is God-breathed and is useful

for instruction,

for conviction,

for correction,

and for training in righteousness,

so that the man of God

may be complete,

fully equipped

for every good work.

2 Timothy 3:16-16 BSB

PART FIVE

The Spiritual Basis of this Book

Whenever God is mentioned in this book, *End-of-Life Spiritual Care,* it refers to the Creator God of Genesis 1:1, the Living God (Elohim Chayim) found in the Bible.

Biblical Judeo-Christian Viewpoint

End-of-Life Spiritual Care is written from a biblical Judeo-Christian viewpoint. The items referenced throughout this book can be used by all denominations and faiths by modifying the rituals and prayers to align with their specific beliefs or denominations. In this way they too will be able to experience the direction and peace their faith provides during their loved one's final days on earth.

> *My soul thirsts for God, for the living God. When shall I come and appear before God? Psalm 42:2 ESV*

And we know that the Son of God has come and has given us understanding, so that we may know Him who is true; and we are in Him who is true—in His Son Jesus Christ. He is the true God and eternal life.
1 John 5:20 BSB

The Judeo-Christian faith believes in the Living God, the God that is alive and active in the lives of those who follow Him. This is the God that we call on during these sacred times, at the hour of our loved one's death.

Yeshua-Jesus

End-of-Life Spiritual Care generally uses the Name 'Yeshua' for 'Jesus.'

Yeshua is the Hebrew Name for Jesus. Jesus is the Name used in the English-speaking world for Yeshua. The full name of 'Yeshua ha Mashiach' is the Hebrew for 'Jesus the Messiah' and "Jesus the Christ" in English.

Both Yeshua and Jesus refer to the Son of God in *End-of-Life Spiritual Care*.

Catholic Guideline

Brief notes from the *Catholic Guidelines for the Dying* are provided for guidance and assurance on performing the spiritual rituals of Confession, Anointing, and Holy Communion which are part of The Last Rites observed by the Catholic Church for those who want or need to perform these rites for their loved one independently.

Your Loved One

The phrase 'your loved one' is used throughout *End-of-Life Spiritual Care* to refer to the one who is dying, the one for whom you are caring. Your loved one can be your spouse, your partner, a parent, a family member, a friend, or in some cases a stranger who needs your help at the end of their life.

Body, Soul, and Spirit

End-of-Life Spiritual Care refers to the body, soul, and spirit when speaking of our life and death. Although they all work together and are complex components of our beings, brief definitions of their individual characteristics are:

Body – The vehicle that your soul and spirit use to live out the physical life you have been given on this Earth.

Soul – The container that holds everything you are and all you have done in this life. This includes the gifts, talents, and abilities you were born with that you use and developed through your works and your deeds, throughout your time on Earth. It holds your memories and accomplishments. It is who you are as an individual. It is and always will be a part of you.

Spirit – The spark within you that gives you life. It is always connected to our Creator, God Almighty. It is energy. It connects your body and soul to the Source, the One Who created them.

'Your loved one' can be

your spouse, your partner,

a parent, a family member,

a friend, or in some cases

a stranger who needs your help

at the end of their life.

Bibliography

Bernard, Jan Selliken, RN. ND and Miriam Schneider, RN, CRNH, *The True Work of Dying,* Avon Books, USA, 1996

Duncan, Katie, NP, *The Dying Process,* USA, 2021

Harman, James T., *Salvation of the Soul,* Prophecy Countdown Publishing, LLC, Maitland, FL, USA 2019

Karnes, Barbara, RN, *The Eleventh Hour,* Barbara Karnes Books, Inc., Vancouver, WA USA, 2008, 2021

Lehnig, Diane, RN, *Midwife to the Other Side,* USA, 2022

Schneider, Miriam, RN, BSN, and Jan Selliken Bernard, RN, BSN, *Midwives to the Dying,* Angel's Work, USA, 1992

Willi, Mary Beth, LPN, *Learning How to Let Go The Signs and Symptoms of the Dying Process*, USA, 2007, 2018, www.learninghowtoletgo.com.
(For a free copy of Mary Beth Willi's booklet, email your request to Rose and she will gladly send you a copy, while supplies are available. Email: SpiritualCareCollection@gmail.com – Subject: Request "Learning" book. Please include your physical mailing info in the email.)

Quotations from CATHOLIC GUIDELINES FOR THE DYING, Schulte, A.J. (1912). Viaticum. In <u>The Catholic Encyclopedia.</u> New York: Robert Appleton Company.

"Although there are many books written about the physical process of dying, I found little written about the spiritual nature of dying from a biblical Judeo-Christian viewpoint or about how to use traditional biblical rituals during the dying process. These lacks are what led me to write this book." ~ Rose Martin

About the Author

The deaths of Rose's parents significantly shaped her insight into life, death, and eternity.

Rose Martin has been a Spirit filled Believer in Yeshua since her life-changing salvation in 1986. She has studied, practiced, and taught the Word of God ever since.

After her father's sudden unexpected death in 1985, Rose earnestly questioned where he went. "What happened to my father? Where did he go?" she seriously wondered.

In her search, she discovered the Jesus of the Bible. She gave her life to Him, was born again on January 3, 1986, and began to regularly attend church along with her husband and children every time the doors were open. The Word of God and serving Him became the main focus of her life.

In her quest to discover more about where her father went when he died, she studied and prayed and found many answers about where we go when we die. She began to speak and teach on the subject and hosted a radio program called "Eternal Life Skills," which aired on OnePlace.com and in several other cities. She authored a book by the same name, *Eternal Life Skills, How to Improve your Life Today While Preparing for Eternity in Heaven,* Rose Martin, 2004, that links our earthly actions with our heavenly life.

Rose was ordained as a Christian minister in 2004 to spread the Word and heal others. In 2008, she was ordained as a Messianic Jewish/Christian Minister.

Rose continued to study and discover how much the Bible reveals about life in Heaven. She began to teach about life in Heaven. Through her ministry she offered a free CD introducing Heaven and how we are preparing for it now. Over a two-year period, this CD went out to over 200 countries blessing over 30,000 people who requested it.

The CD led her to write and produce a show called, "Exploring Life in Heaven with Rose Martin." She presented it at The Nova Theater in Branson, Missouri from 2005-2007. People were blessed by the colorful, hopeful, biblical interpretation of what life is like in Heaven and learned how they can live their current life preparing for it.

Tremendous insight into life on Earth and the life in Heaven came while sitting vigil at her mother's bedside for the week leading up to her death on Easter Sunday, 2022. The Holy Spirit allowed Rose to spiritually see the spiritual activity involved in the process of transitioning from our earthly body to our heavenly life.

Bible verses started coming to mind that matched what she saw in the spiritual. Each day she experienced an increasing love of God that orchestrated the entire process. She began to understand how we get from 'here' to 'there.'

Rose's mother was a devout Roman Catholic Believer, and so Rose included some of the spiritual rituals that were part of her mother's faith, such as prayer, worship, anointing oil, and a prayer scarf. She believes this, along with the loving support she had from her family, helped set the spiritual atmosphere for her mother to make a most peaceful transition, and for her family to be at peace also.

In this book, *End-of-Life Spiritual Care: Spiritual Insights and Biblical Rituals to Help Your Loved One Step into Eternity with Faith, Love, and Dignity*, Rose shares the insight she received about the spiritual aspect of the dying process during her mother's transition to eternity, along with what she has learned since.

Rose also gives examples of prayers and ceremonies for families to easily create a sacred space for their loved one in which the labor of dying can take place.

Rose hopes that *End-of-Life Spiritual Care* will help others understand their loved one's transition to eternity better, and make it a most meaningful experience, both for the departing and the loved ones that remain. She also believes that it will help those who are grieving the loss of their loved one to better understand what they experienced and to be assured that they are safe.

~~~~~~~~~~~

Rose currently lives in Northwest Arkansas with her husband of 38 years, Charles, and their two Chinese Crested Hairless/Morkie mix fur'less' babies.

Contact her at SpiritualCareCollection@gmail.com.

Other books by Rose Martin

Discovering Your God-Given Identity, 2021

Your Destiny Discovered, 2020

Exploring Life in Heaven with Rose Martin, 2004

Eternal Life Skills, How to Improve Your Life Today While Preparing for Life in Heaven, 2004

Thank you for reading this book!

I hope you have been blessed by this book and that it
has given you and your loved one comfort and
guidance throughout this very special time.

If you have been helped and believe this book would
be beneficial to others who's loved one has recently
passed, or who are going through this transition
with their loved one now, or whose loved one has
already passed on, please let them know about it!

One way you can help others find this book is by
writing an online review, or email it to us
and we may post it on our website!

Thank you very much!

Our Contact Info:

SpiritualCareCollection@gmail.com
www.End-of-Life-Spiritual-Care.com

Spiritual Care Collection

Colorful items for use with your End-of-Life Ceremony

~ Spiritual Care Collection ~

Your choice of...

Prayer Shawl
or Tallit*

*colors and patterns vary

Spiritual Care Collection

Designed for your convenience - all the items used in the End-of-Life Ceremony in one collection to use in your special times with your loved one!

Each Spiritual Care Collection* is individually assembled and includes:

Your choice of either –
1 – Women's Prayer Scarf OR
1 – Men's or Women's Tallit
    (Messianic Jewish/Christian style)

Plus...
1 – Vile of unscented anointing oil
1 – Bowl for water
7 – Self-contained communion cups with wafer
1 – 2" Unscented wax candle in a votive
1 – Battery operated candle
1 – Gold votive for the battery candle
1 – Black tote bag, journal, and pen
1 – Step-by-step instructions

*Colors and styles may vary depending on stock and availability when ordered.

**Visit www.SpiritualCareCollection.com
to check availability and select your collection!**

We come into the world

on our own and

we leave the world on our own.

Dying is a journey

each person must

ultimately make alone

when it is their time.

Even so, people want and need their

family and friends with them to help

them make the transition.

Bless you for being that friend!

*Let others know how they can help
their loved one too! Share:*

www.End-of-Life-Spiritual-Care.com

Notes:

Notes:

Made in the USA
Columbia, SC
15 February 2023

12139301R00096